THE Barralong ADVENTURE

a memoir by
GLENN GORDON STOTT

Copyright ©2024 Glenn Gordon Stott

All rights reserved.

No part of this book may be reproduced in any form or by any electronic or mechanical means, including information storage and retrieval systems, without permission in writing from the author, except by reviewers, who may quote brief passages in a review.

For inquiries please contact:
Elaine Ash/Glenn Stott
6444 E. Spring Street
Unit 149
Long Beach, CA 90815

Cover and Interior Design: Derin Chisel
Editor and Publishing Consultant: Elaine Ash

ISBN: 9798864483909

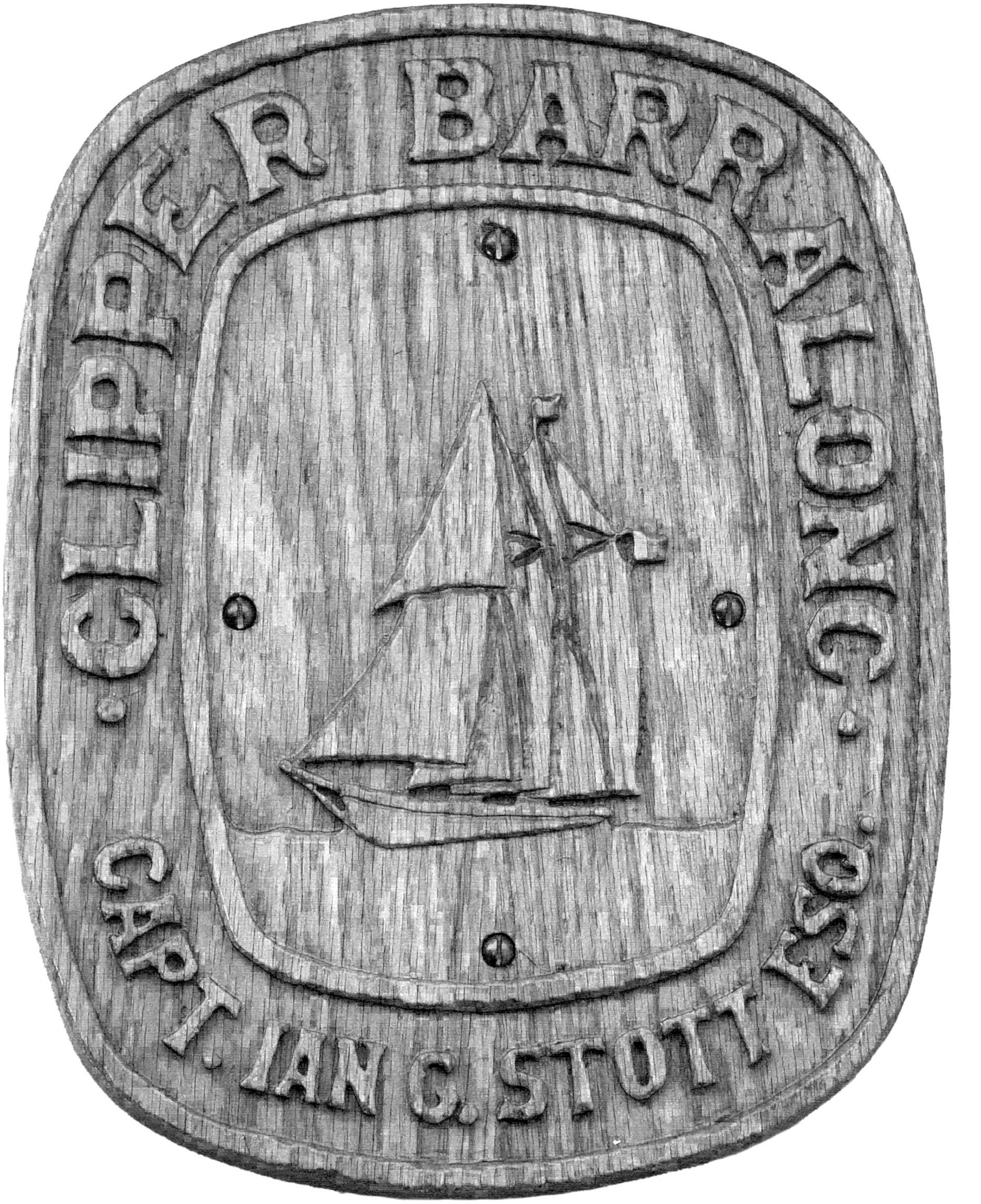
CLIPPER BARRALONG
CAPT. IAN G. STOTT ESQ.

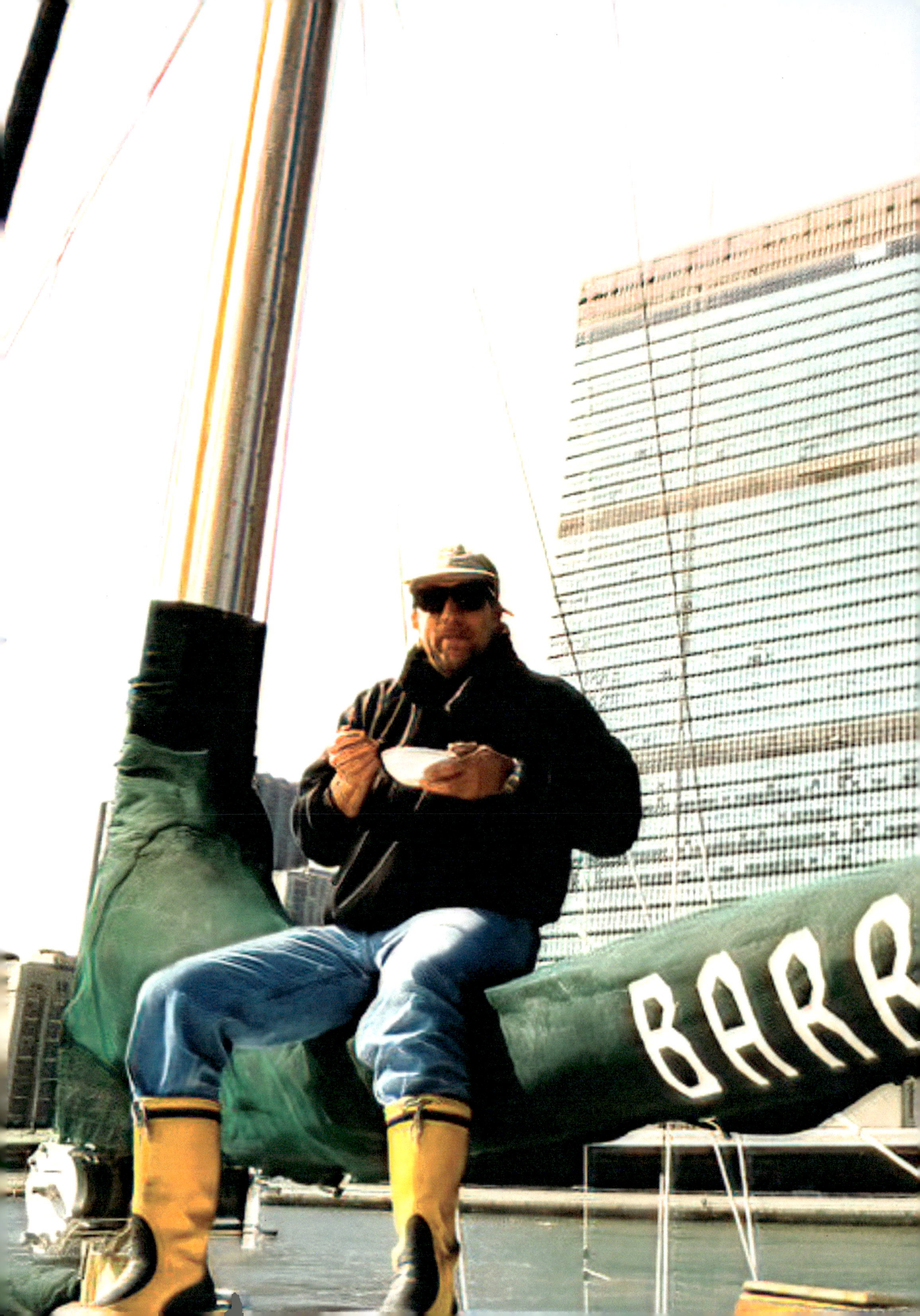
BARR

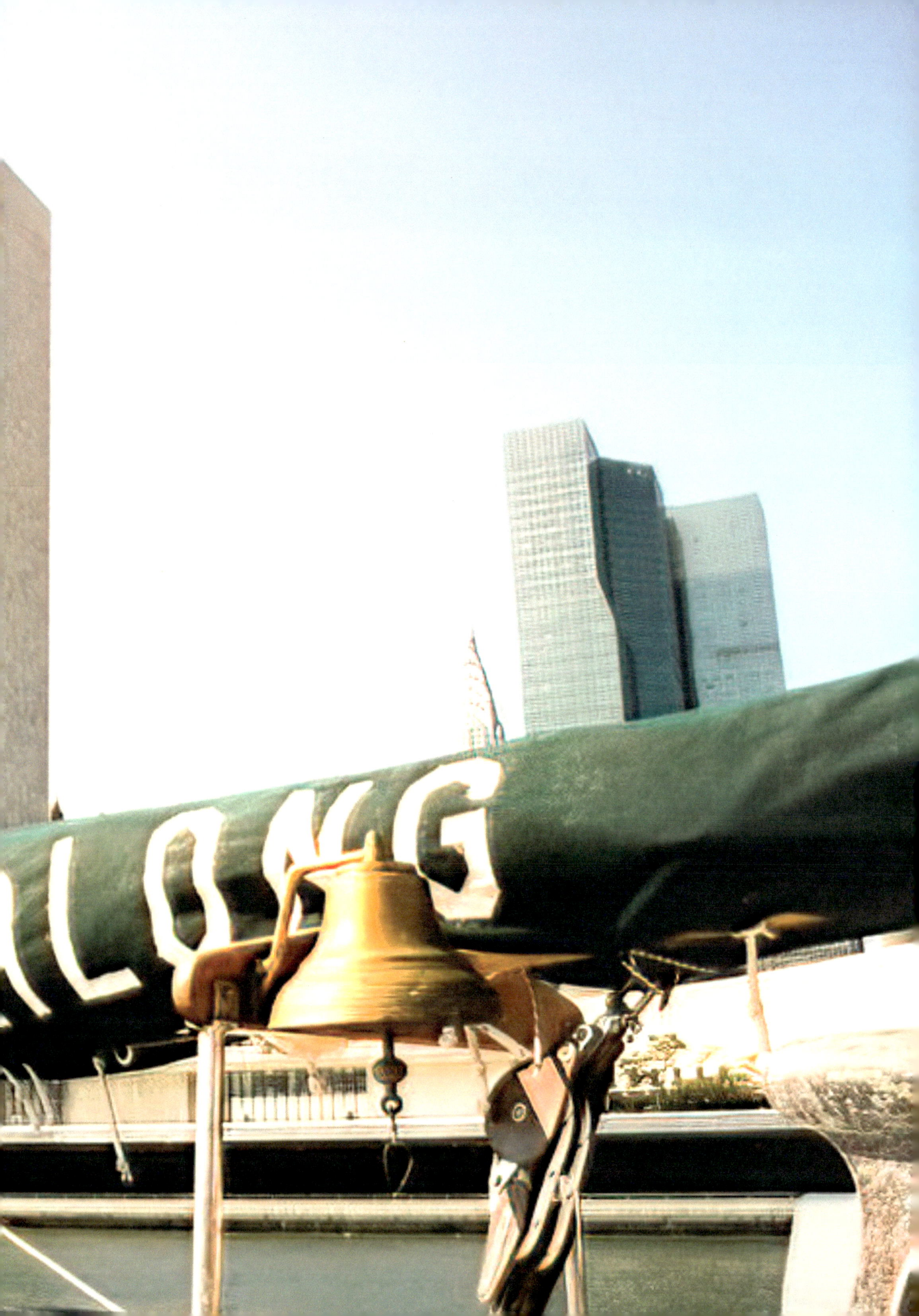
LONG

TABLE OF CONTENTS

Dedication by Brean Stott...........12

Foreword by Steve Teatro...........14

Introduction by Ian Stott, Jr...........15

Chapter One: From Scotland to Canada...........17

Chapter Two: The *Alacrity* and Other Watery Stories...........25

Chapter Three: Replacing the *Silver Sharon*, and the Bacardi Cup...........39

Chapter Four: Passing of a Patriarch—The Death of Ian Gordon Stott, Sr...........50

Chapter Five: Future of the *Barralong*...........53

Chapter Six: St. Peter's to Halifax...........70

Chapter Seven: Sails Set for Nantucket—Adventure on the High Seas...........81

Chapter Eight: New Haven to New Jersey
Disaster Strikes with a Surprise Ending...........89

Appendix: Pictures, Documents and Memories...........102
    For Mariners Only—Technical & Mechanical Details...........114

Acknowledgements...........129

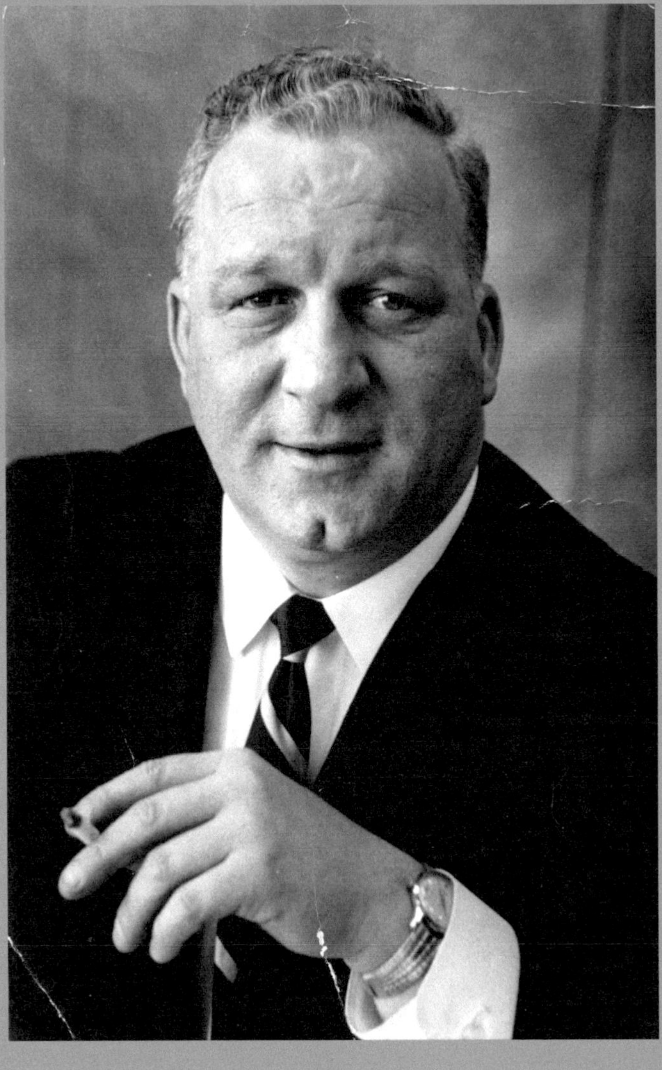

DEDICATION

I would like to thank my brother Glenn for all the time and effort that went into writing this book. What a wonderful dedication to the memory of our father. Glenn and Dad are people who accomplish seemingly impossible tasks with sheer determination and a force of will.

The *Barralong* meant the world to my father and the ship was his "baby." Most visits to Islandview started with casual conversation, sharing a drink, but almost always ended up onboard the *Barralong*. Sometimes conversations got heated. I knew I was grown up when an argument finally went my way. I miss those days!

Dad was a true entrepreneur. He found ways to help with the *Barralong*'s expenses by negotiating sail-training contracts with the Navy cadets. He got paid to teach young cadets the seamanship skills he'd mastered, and loved every minute of it.

My favourite picture of Dad is at the wheel of the *Barralong* with a rum in hand. He was truly in his element.

Ian Gordon Stott passed away before my kids were born. How I wish Alexandra and Breanna got a chance to meet their grandfather. They missed out on hearing the stories only he could tell. They may not have met you, Dad, but they miss you! Also, thanks for raising us to believe that anything is possible if you work hard enough.

When I went out partying in my late teens, Dad always reminded me to "remember the day and the date." That's a memory I cherish to this day.

Cheers,

Brean Stott
Sydney, Nova Scotia
March, 2023

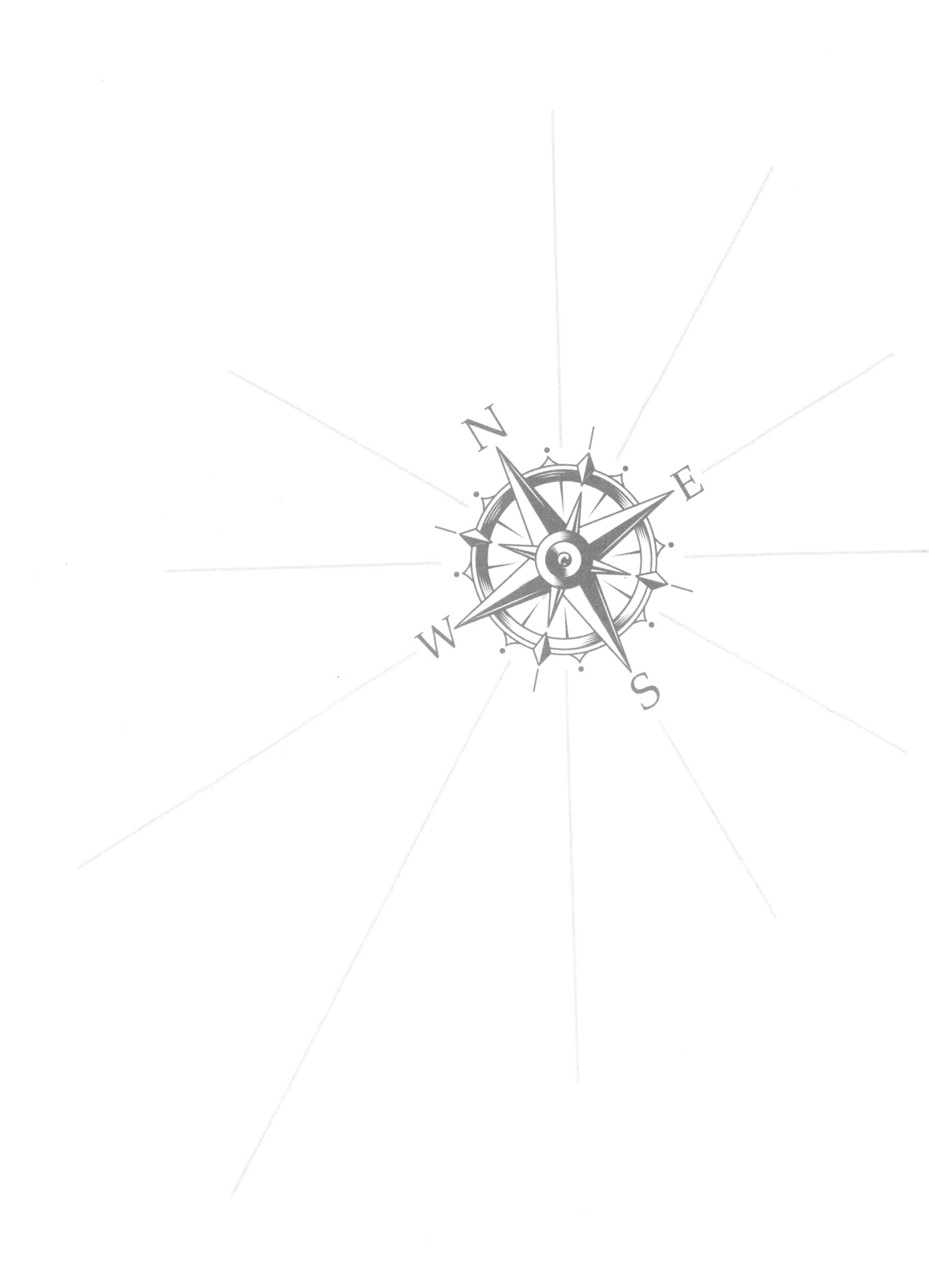

FOREWORD

I first met Glenn Stott while we were both serving as Royal Canadian Air Force pilots stationed at 15 Wing in Moose Jaw, Saskatchewan. Glenn and I were flying as Wing maintenance test pilots and serving as operations officers at the Wing.

In 1993 while flying together to perform at the Rhode Island International Airshow, we diverted to Sydney, Nova Scotia where I first laid eyes on the *Barralong* moored in her boathouse. Stories told by both Glenn and his brother, Brean, introduced me to the wonderful adventures of Ian Stott and the *Barralong*.

In 2012, almost twenty years later, I was once again reunited with Glenn. This time we were aboard my own sailboat, the Jabiroo II, on the west coast of Canada where I met Glenn's mother and sister, and heard more stories about Cape Breton, boys, boats, and the *Barralong*.

My wife Ginny and I have been living and cruising aboard Jabiroo II for ten years and have sailed over 15,000 miles since we left Victoria, Canada.

Part of Ian Stott's legacy lies in the *Barralong* and her adventures. Glenn has done a great service by memorializing the stories in this book. As time marches on, our memories will begin to fade. But this memoir and the adventures described will be read and kept alive by the nieces, the nephews, the grandchildren of Ian, and future generations to come.

—Steve Teatro

Skipper, Jabiroo II
Former RCAF Squadron Commander,
President of Showline Airshows, and
Executive Director, San Francisco Fleet Week Airshow

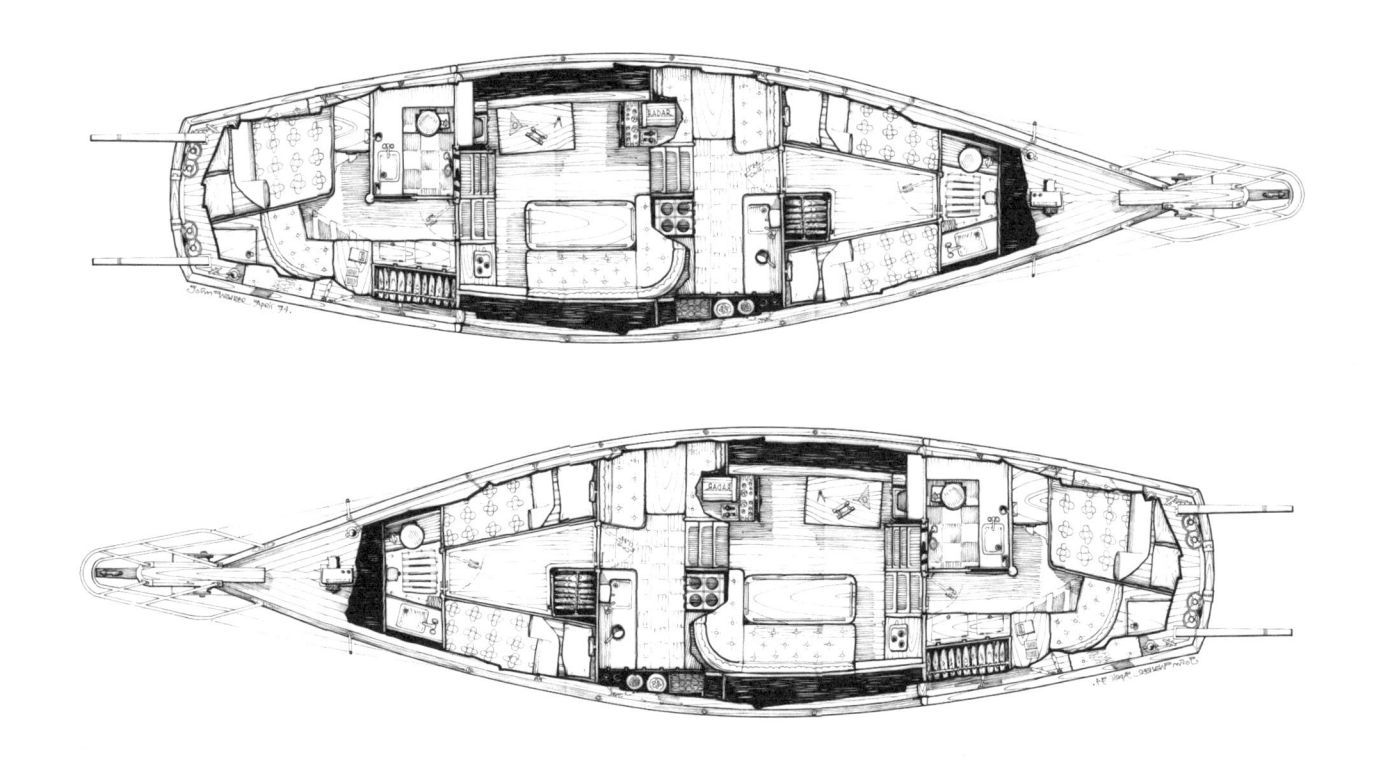

INTRODUCTION BY IAN STOTT, JR.

In 1985 my father, Ian Gordon Stott, purchased the *Barralong* sailing vessel. She was an amazing boat—Dutch built, steel hull, twin marine Volvo diesel engines. She served Dad, his companies, and our family well for many years. After Dad passed in 1995 it was time to sell. The *Barralong* wasn't a superyacht and didn't absolutely require a broker to handle the sale. My brothers, Glenn and Brean, decided to do it themselves and, I mean, how many times do you sell a yacht? It was a once in a lifetime thing.

Glenn, as co-executor of Dad's estate, was tasked with that job —finding a buyer, negotiating the deal, and making delivery. His responsibilities entailed planning the navigation from Nova Scotia to whatever corner of the world her new owner lived in; planning, permits, resupplying food, fuel and necessities, assembling a competent crew, and assuring their safety. Thankfully, Glenn had everything he needed in terms of skill from selling to sailing, and acting as captain of the *Barralong*.

Eleanor Roosevelt said that great leaders inspire people to have confidence in themselves. After Glenn found a buyer in Virginia, he needed the kind of leadership Eleanor Roosevelt was talking about. Almost the minute they sailed out of the Bras d'Or saltwater lake, the *Barralong* was hit with everything from a hurricane and treacherous seas, freezing weather, crew seasickness, supply shortages, and know-nothing marina bureaucrats in charge of life and death situations.

Mariners generally fear and avoid the North Atlantic in October for good reason. Glenn used his natural leadership ability to inspire the crew and keep them motivated while working through the multiple adversities they encountered on the high seas. A lot of adventures happened sailing from Bras d'Or to Halifax, and then on to New York and Virginia.

So sit back, gentle readers, and enjoy this high-stakes tale of a sailing vessel with its human adventure. My most important contribution to the book is to point out the part that Glenn played, and to make sure he knows how grateful we all are for the job he saw through.

— Ian Stott, Jr.
Moncton, New Brunswick
October, 2022

Chapter ONE

From Scotland to Canada

In 1940 my grandmother, a nurse and driver for the local hospital, wrestled a large ambulance through the shipyards of Grangemouth, Scotland. She struggled to steer because all sources of light, including her headlights, were restricted to prevent the German Luftwaffe from pinpointing bombing targets. To make matters worse, the ambulance was a standard stick shift, built long before automatic transmissions, power steering, and power brakes were invented. Suddenly, the front tire hit a curb and the steering wheel was wrenched violently from her grip. Her hands and forearms ached each time the front tires struck something but she had to keep going—many lives were at stake.

At last she turned into the hospital yard where emergency services personnel were waiting. Nurse Kilgour's adventure finished as the last of the injured people were whisked from the back of her ambulance to emergency medical treatment.

Elspet Rennie Stott, née Kilgour, 1943 *Frank (Pop) Stott, MBE*

Elspet Rennie Kilgour was born in the Scottish Highlands on Christmas Day of 1902. I'm told she matured into a beautiful young woman with piercing blue eyes, platinum blond hair, and the regal posture of a Celtic princess. In stark contrast, her boyfriend and future husband, Frank Stott, later known as Pop Stott, was a tall, burly blacksmith with jet-black hair. Years later Elspet became a nursing supervisor and Frank a skilled foreman in the shipyards of Grangemouth, a small industrial town on the banks of the River Forth. The Stott family came from humble beginnings but my grandparents decided their children Frank Jr., Doreen, and Ian would have something better.

Young Ian, for example, wanted to be a lawyer. Pop Stott started his career as a blacksmith by trade but was later hired by the Grangemouth shipyards due to his superior metallurgy skills. When World War II started, Pop was already an experienced shipbuilding foreman so he was branded as essential to the war effort. Much to his dismay, Pop was not allowed to join the fight and was ordered to stay in Grangemouth and supervise the repair of damaged ships and submarines.

Ian and his mother Elspet

Their three young children; Frank Jr., Doreen, and Ian suffered through the stigma of having their able-bodied father perceived as a sickly coward by local children. Many women in Grangemouth were envious of Elspet because her husband came home every night while they prayed anxiously for the safety of their husbands fighting at the battlefront. Grangemouth had become a frequent Luftwaffe target because it also had a training facility for Allied fighter pilots, and a refinery.

As soon as he was eligible my uncle Frank Jr. enlisted in the RAF as a gunner and wireless operator. In 1943 my father, Ian, was still only fourteen when he begged Pop Stott to vouch for him as being sixteen so he could join the war effort. When Pop reluctantly agreed, Dad immediately enlisted in the navy and was commissioned as a sublieutenant, all before he was 16. He would have spent his career in the Navy but when the war ended Pop reached in and pulled him out. Dad's destiny was to study and become a lawyer. Pop was destined to be awarded an MBE (Member of the British Empire) medal for gallantry by King George VI.

Gran and Pop, January 25th, 1970, at the Caledonian Society's 211th celebration of Robbie Burns, the famous Scottish poet

Shortly after the war the Stott family emigrated to Montreal, Canada. Pop was snapped up by the Dofasco Steel Company for his knowledge of metallurgy, and Dad attended law school while working evenings in a restaurant. A frequent diner there struck up a conversation about the incredible growth and opportunities in the emerging aluminum building products industry. The diner was the president of Weather Products Corp based in Warwick, Rhode Island. After several conversations Dad accepted a very generous offer to move to the United States.

Dad was a top performer and within two years rose to become the vice president of international marketing for the Weather Products Corporation. He did receive his law degree but never practiced law. Dad made a deal to return to Nova Scotia and become the VP of a new Weather Products Corp subsidiary in Canada. Six years later he owned it.

At the same time, Dad started Stott Aluminum in 1952. He thought the best market for aluminum windows would be in Scotland and England because of his design and installation experience with the harsh Canadian climate. Stott Aluminum windows were vastly superior to those available in Europe so he landed some substantial contracts to ship windows to Britain. One of his customers was a prefab builder called Swift Homes, and a Swift home was chosen by Woman's Magazine for a national award. Its most desirable feature, said the magazine, was its double-glazed windows from Stott Aluminum Corporation of Sydney, Nova Scotia.

The multinationals started to take notice. Alcan was the largest aluminum company in the world, spending millions to gain a foothold in the European building products market. Meanwhile this fellow from Nova Scotia was already exporting to Europe and drawing media attention. Alcan asked if he would come and work for them. Dad said yes but only if he had equity in the new company. No, said Alcan, nobody but Alcan owned shares in its subsidiaries.

In 1969, after a series of difficult negotiations, Dad was permitted to buy twenty-five percent of Alcan Design Products Ltd, of which he became managing director and chief executive officer. Stott Aluminum had the management contract, so in late 1969 we moved to Northampton, England. My brother Brean and I went to school in Northampton while the new 12,000-square-foot factory was gearing up for production.

During the next ten years, Dad rose to chairman and CEO, and oversaw the expansion of five factories, 87 branches, 4,000 dealers, 5,000 direct and about 12,000 indirect employees. After a year we moved back to Nova Scotia but Dad was spending two weeks out of every five in England. It was incredible—Alcan Design Products was doing $140 million dollars annually.

We moved back to Nova Scotia after a year in Northampton. During the mid-1970s Dad established new Canadian businesses in the hardwood lumber industry, a weekly newspaper, apartment buildings, shipping, and real estate.

Finding Our Home

The name for the province of Nova Scotia is derived from a Gaelic name meaning New Scotland. At the northeastern tip of Nova Scotia is Cape Breton Island which is famous for its Scottish culture and traditional fiddle music. Like Scotland, Cape Breton is composed of rocky shores, rolling farmland, glacial valleys, barren headlands, highlands, woods, and plateaus. Dad loved Cape Breton and decided to create a home here. Cape Breton only accounts for 18.7% of Nova Scotia's total land area but at the turn of the century it was at the forefront of scientific advancements led by the activities of inventors Alexander Graham Bell and Guglielmo Marconi.

In 1969 Dad purchased fifty acres for $800 on the shore of the Bras d'Or Lake at Islandview, Cape Breton. Here he built his dream home and called it Highgate House. The views were magnificent and it had two huge fireplaces, a well-stocked wine cellar, stables, a guest house, two boathouses, and a 300-foot wharf in the perfectly protected cove that served as a private harbour.

Dad split from my mother Gloria in 1968. I was nine and Brean was eight, so we stayed with him in Cape Breton. Our siblings, Kirk age seven, Sheila age five, and Moira age one, moved to New Brunswick to live with Gloria. Dad's son Ian Jr., from a previous marriage, was living in Yarmouth, Nova Scotia.

Brean and I moved to Highgate House in 1972 so we were introduced to boating and country life at an early age. Brean became a successful businessman and took over Stott Aluminum in 1984. I joined the Royal Canadian Air Force to fly jets and then the C-130 Hercules. Mom worked as a registered nurse in Moncton and Victoria, British Columbia. Kirk became a boat captain in Kelowna and Sheila worked for the health department in Victoria. Moira and her husband Ross raised two sons in their beautiful log cabin home in Port Moody, BC.

When dad passed away unexpectedly on August 6th, 1995, he left behind a wealth of colorful memories and anecdotes. This story is about his family, his beloved sailboat the *Barralong*, and other marine-related adventures.

Previous Boats and Other Tales

In 1965 we lived in a residential neighbourhood in Sydney, Nova Scotia. When my brother Brean was four or five years old he suddenly went missing after supper and the family looked everywhere for him. Dad called the police and the neighbours formed search teams, but they still hadn't found him by nightfall. Eventually someone found him fast asleep laying across the front seat of the speedboat in our garage. The garage had been previously searched and nobody knows how his short little legs climbed up over the trailer and into the speedboat, but he did. I'll never forget when Mom and Dad asked him why he did it. Brean explained it as only a five-year-old could—he wanted to sit in the driver's seat—grabbed the steering wheel, and started bouncing up and down making motorboat sounds until he fell fast asleep.

Brean and the Speedboat

Ten years later in 1975 we were living at Highgate House when Dad arrived home from work and noticed that his new speedboat was not at the dock. He asked, "Where is my speedboat?" Brean replied that he parked it at Mary McIntyre's house. Dad read him the riot act about responsibility and told him the boat belonged here. He yelled, "Go and get my speedboat and tie it up at our dock where it belongs."

It was my job to drive Brean to Mary's house and drop him off. Mary lived five miles down the lake so it should have taken less than thirty minutes to get home. After an hour we all wondered what was taking him. It would be dark soon so I called Mary and she said Brean left hours ago. She added that the boat almost sank earlier that afternoon and they barely made it to shore. They had recently watched the James Bond movie, *Live and Let Die* with its incredible scenes of boats jumping over a narrow sandbar at high speed. The theory was that if you trimmed up the outboard motor and the boat was going fast enough, you could launch over a sandbar.

Brean allegedly tried that maneuver several times without success. What he didn't realize was that the abrasive sand and gravel gradually wore a hole through the fiberglass hull. The hole was in the bow so if he went fast enough to stay on plane, the hole stayed above the water. As the boat slowed down and the bow dropped below the surface, the hole filled with water.

At ten p.m. we called the Royal Canadian Mounted Police and the Coast Guard. They searched the coastline but there was no sign of Brean. Dad was still out searching when the RCMP picked him up at two a.m. Apparently the speedboat sank close to shore so Brean tied the rope to a tree. It then took him several hours to climb through the woods toward the highway to start walking home. After he arrived home, the search was called off. The next day he was promptly demoted from the seafaring Captain Brean, to just plain old Brean.

Chapter TWO

The *Alacrity* & Other Watery Stories

Alacrity

Our first sailboat, purchased in 1971, was a 24-foot sloop called *Alacrity*. She had twin bilge keels—which are two shorter keels rather than one long one—that allowed the boat to reach shallower water and still provide enough stability for sailing.

In shallow water, a sailboat with a single keel will fall over on its side at low tide and fill with water when the tide returns. The twin bilge keel design featured two keels emerging at an angle from the bottom so a sailboat could stay upright in shallow water. When the tide went out, the boat would sit on her keels and remain stable and upright. The design was created for rivers and coastal areas that experienced extreme changes in tide, like the Mersey River in England, and the Fundy tides of Atlantic Canada. I found out later that the name *Alacrity* means "eagerness."

In the early 1970s we didn't have a dock or a mooring ball in the pond to park the *Alacrity*. In those days a mooring was made from two engine blocks chained together through the piston holes. Old engine blocks were much cheaper and easier to find in Cape Breton so they were usually used instead of expensive mushroom anchors. A section of heavy chain with one-inch-thick links connected the engine blocks to another section of much lighter chain that connected to a buoy on the surface. When a boat secured to a mooring buoy pitched in stormy weather, it pulled the chain tight before any force was applied to the engine blocks. Each pull lifted the heavy chain off the bottom which acted like a shock absorber.

To create such a mooring, Dad lowered two, heavy engine blocks into a small wooden dingy so it sat extremely low in the water. Once the dinghy was towed to the proper position, a paddle would be used to tip the dinghy over and release the engines. One overlooked detail was that much of the rusty chain and the buoy were still in the inflatable boat that was used to tow the dinghy. The pond was covered in thick weeds and the bottom was very muddy so an outboard motor couldn't be used for towing. Dad rowed the inflatable to the perfect spot and then flipped the dinghy.

Everything was going according to plan until the engines pulled the chain from the floor of the inflatable. The rusty chain, pulled into the water by the sinking engines, acted like a chain saw and tore the inflatable in half. Dad was covered in weeds as he struggled to swim to shore but couldn't stand up in the shallow water because of the muddy bottom. He was covered in muck and seaweeds as he crawled and rolled up onto dry land. I was twelve or thirteen at the time and watched the whole thing from the shoreline. I'd never seen anything so funny and tried not to laugh, but every time I looked at him I couldn't hold it in. He was annoyed and not the least bit amused but at least we now had a mooring.

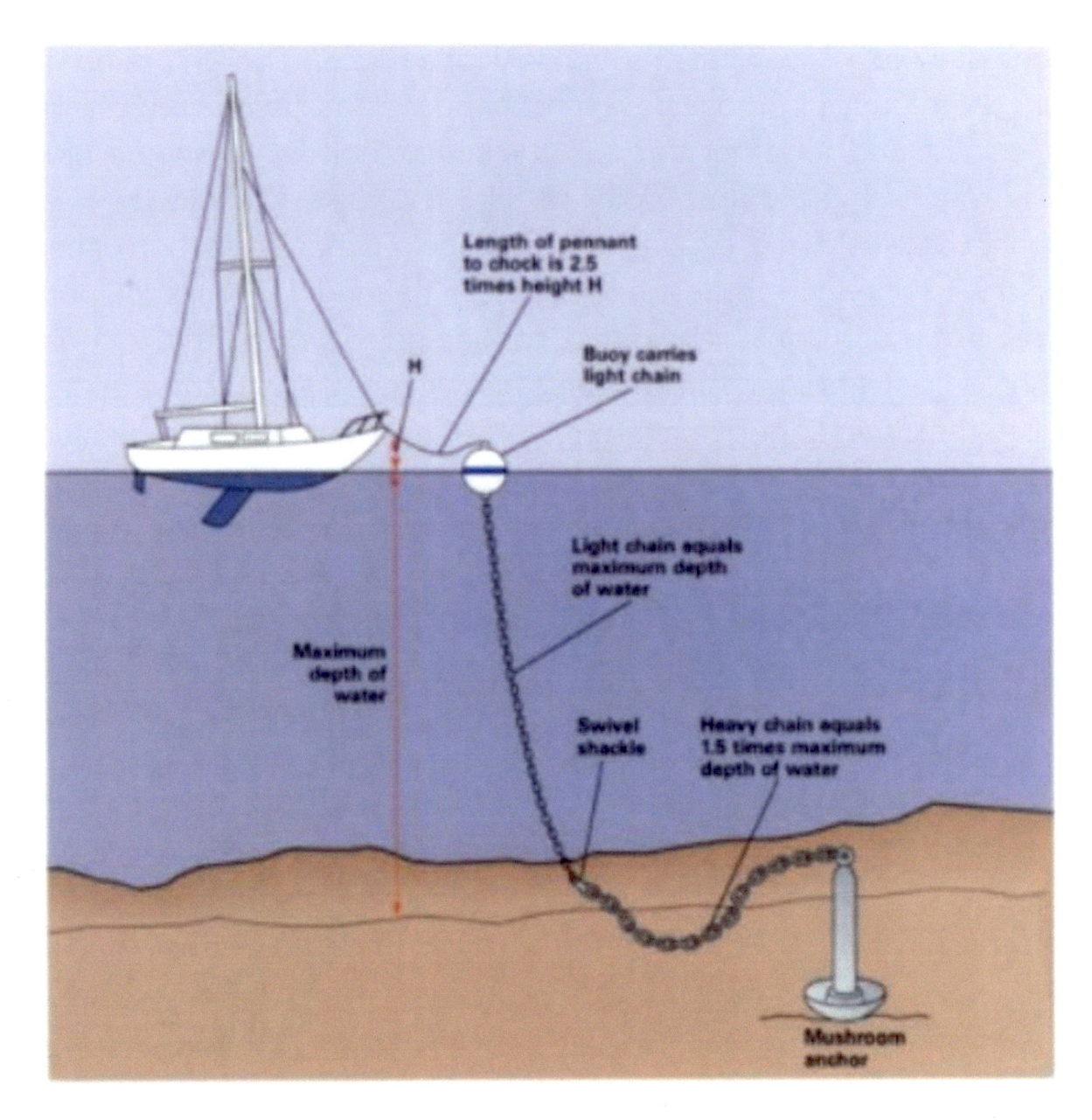

- Heavy chain = 1.5 x depth of water
- Heavy chain joined to light chain via swivel shackle
- Length of small chain = Maximum Depth of water
- Buoy carries light chain
- Length of pennant from buoy to chock = 2.5 x height of freeboard

Image courtesy of Chapman Piloting Seamanship & Small Boat Handling

How to set up a mooring

That new mooring kept the *Alacrity* safe in the pond for many years. She was very stable and the perfect craft for beginners. Dad later sold it to Mack Read, a neighbour who lived five miles down the lake. After the money was exchanged, Dad, Mack, and several large friends piled aboard the *Alacrity* for the delivery. There was lots of wind so they decided to "see what she could do." Suddenly the mast snapped in two places, covering them in sails and rigging so the disabled craft had to be towed back to Mack's property by speedboat. As Dad stepped onto Mack's wharf he allegedly turned to him and said, "Good luck with it!"

MV *Silver Sharon*

This 35-foot, twin-masted ketch replaced the *Alacrity* and was built of oak and teak by J. A. Silver of Greenock, Scotland. One of my first memories of the *Silver Sharon* was Joe Capstick and his crane trying to lift it out of the pond for the winter. The *Sharon* weighed only ten tons or thereabouts, but Joe's 25-ton crane couldn't lift it because the boom needed to extend too far out over the water.

Dad decided to build a marine railway on the ice and let it settle to the bottom when the ice melted. That way the *Sharon* could be pulled up onshore before the winter using a railway-car cradle. It sounded like a great idea and the day we tried it everything was working well as we watched more of the hull emerge from the water. At some point the full weight of the boat was supported by the cradle which forced the right-side rail to sink into the soft muddy bottom. The *Sharon* was strapped to the railcar and listing steeply but Dad was determined to pull it all the way out. The boat and cradle almost toppled sideways into the water before he finally had to give up on the idea.

After Brean's speedboat incident Dad was concerned about allowing us to take his sailboat by ourselves. We were now semi-responsible teenagers with driver's licenses but the *Silver Sharon* was a much larger and expensive responsibility. Neither of us kids could afford to repair or replace it so Dad

Joe Capstick and his crane carry the Silver Sharon in a sling

created a series of lessons to ensure we could handle it safely.
I don't know why specifically, but Dad never let my brother Brean take it out alone with his friends. I do remember that Brean thought the lessons were an unnecessary bother. I'm sure the fact that he had already wrecked a few cars and sank the speedboat probably factored heavily into Dad's decision.

I had some great times on *Silver Sharon*, though. One summer we attempted to pick up some friends a few miles down the lake for a teenager sailboat party. Most of the narrow docks are built from two-by-fours for a canoe or small speedboat so they're much too shallow for the *Silver Sharon* to safely come alongside. The plan was to inch forward to the end of the dock and have the passengers climb up over the bow. There were so many kids aboard already that they blocked the view of the dock from the wheelhouse. Graham Moffatt stood on the bow and yelled directions as the *Sharon* steamed purposefully toward the dock full of teens eager to join the party.

A teenager party aboard the Silver Sharon

As I forged ahead Graham announced, "Keep coming, keep coming, a little more." Suddenly Graham yelled, "Ok, hold it!" The bow was only six inches from the dock. CRUNCH! The ten-ton sailboat plowed through the deck resulting in lots of floating debris and fully clothed swimmers splashing frantically to round up their belongings before they sank.

George Swan (aka Swanny)

Swanny from North Sydney was Dad's longtime friend and a descendant of the giantess Anna Swan. When Anna was four years old she was almost five feet tall and continued growing to eight feet tall in adulthood. In the 1800s she was known as the tallest woman in the world and toured for P.T. Barnum. In contrast, Swanny was only five-foot-six and owned several clothing stores.

One pitch-black night about two a.m., Swanny was at the helm, steaming from Baddeck to Islandview when we suddenly ground to a halt on a shoal. We were hard aground but the engine alone didn't have enough power in reverse to pull us free. Dad grabbed the controls and Swanny jumped into the water to help push us off the shoal. He was in water up to his chin and grunting with effort, while the engine churned away in reverse at full throttle.

Brean, Liz (Dad's current wife), and I were now wide awake and Dad told us to walk from one side of the boat to the other. The shifting weight of everybody moving from side to side was supposed to set up a rocking motion that would hopefully help wiggle the boat free. Suddenly the boat broke free and accelerated away rapidly into the night. We were free of the shoal but where was Swanny? When he left the shoal to swim toward us we'd lost track of him.

We frantically scanned the blackness for any sign of him but our flashlights weren't powerful enough. We couldn't get too close to his last known position or we'd run aground again. The waves were small but just big enough to obscure his bobbing head and it was hard to hear anything over the sound of the engine. To make matters worse, Swanny wasn't wearing a brightly colored lifejacket and had jet-black hair. He initially had a lifejacket, but his short legs couldn't get enough traction on the lake bottom while wearing it. Brean and I were genuinely concerned when it took so long to find him because the adults had taken a fair amount to drink.

The Bras d'Or Lake is huge. It was over 400 square miles in size, with tides and currents, and a maximum depth of 942 feet. Eventually we decided to shut down the engine and yelled out to him. A short time later we found Swanny, to everyone's great relief. He was thoroughly exhausted and didn't have enough strength left to get back aboard on his own.

Marine Railway

After the botched railway idea at Islandview, Dad decided to haul out the *Sharon* at the Dobson Yacht Club. Each October, Joe would lift the *Sharon* onto her railway cradle, and Brean and I would repaint the hull and brightwork the following spring. There was a heavy canvas tarp over the boat to protect her from the snow, so in April of 1975 Brean and I drove there to remove the tarp and bring it home. I'll never forget that day because we had a brand-new green Mazda 808 station wagon and the ink on my driver's license was barely two weeks old.

The tarp was really heavy so the plan was to roll it back toward the stern and then reverse the station wagon up to the rear of the cradle. Then we would let the tarp drop to the ground, open the rear door, and stuff it all into the back of the car. Brean was only fifteen and was itching to reverse the car into the final position.

At first it wouldn't start because it was a standard shift. The clutch pedal had to be pushed all the way in to start it. He knew enough to shift into reverse but each time he stepped on the gas, the engine revved up but the car didn't move. I could hear the *vroom, vroom* of the engine at high RPM and yelled out to him to stop. He must have suddenly let the clutch out too fast and the Mazda rocketed back into the *Sharon* at nearly full throttle. It struck the steel rudder which sliced through the car's rear door like a meat cleaver.

To make matters worse, Brean still had it in gear so the rear wheels were spinning. Luckily the *Sharon* was ten tons and the modified railway car was many more tons, so nothing moved or fell over. I rushed down off the boat to confront Brean but he took off and ran through the yacht club with me screaming in hot pursuit. He hid in a bathroom stall and I was trying to kick the door in when suddenly I was grabbed from behind and lifted until my feet left the ground. Lester Fleet had been at the bar and ran after us to see what the commotion was all about. He dragged me by the scruff of the neck out of the bathroom and demanded an explanation. When I told him what happened he checked out the car and said it was still drivable.

When my father saw the damage he told me I would have to claim responsibility and say I was confused by the gears because Brean didn't have a license.

Backhoe Incident

The Islandview property required a considerable amount of maintenance each year. We had a backhoe for clearing the winter snow and to assist with heavy maintenance during the summer. It was very powerful compared to a lawn-mower tractor and was great for earth moving, digging, and towing things. One winter the pack ice seized into the dock pilings and the rising tides under the ice shifted the height of some of the poles. The dock surface was uneven so a pile driver was needed to pound the higher pilings back down to the same level as the others.

Dad told me to drive the backhoe onto the dock and use the rear arm as a battering ram to pound the poles back into position. I tried to remind him that the backhoe weighed at least 15,000 pounds and could not be supported by the thin planking on the dock. He was furious at my refusal and stormed off with the backhoe keys to do it himself. He was never good with machinery so I rushed into the boathouse to gather some sheets of three-quarter-inch plywood to lay down over the planks in an effort to spread out the weight.

He was yelling and in a hurry as I ran up onto the dock to direct him slowly back toward the first pole. When the backhoe crashed through the wharf into the lake I barely managed to leap onto an adjacent dock section. The big machine was still running and the top of the engine compartment was peeking up from the water's surface. Dad was up to his chest in water screaming, "Get it out, get it out, GET IT OUT!!" I scrambled down onto the backhoe to feel for the controls but the engine died and it was truly stuck. Joe Capstick was called but he couldn't get his big crane out to Islandview until the next day.

Overnight the backhoe sank further into the muddy bottom and now the muck had a really strong grip on it. A 75-ton crane can lift a 75-ton load when the load is positioned close to it, but that wasn't the case here. The farther the crane had to reach its long arm out over the water the less stable the crane became and the less it could lift. It ended up taking both a 75-ton crane and a tractor-trailer tow truck to extract it. The crane provided a lifting force while the tow truck slowly dragged it through the mud toward the body of the crane on dry land.
This whole operation drew a crowd of onlookers up along the highway, as each passing vehicle stopped to see what was going on. Once the muddy backhoe was close to the crane, it was easily lifted onto a flatbed truck and whisked away, never to be seen again. At the same time, Dad had a swarm of carpenters fix the dock and acted like the whole incident never happened.

Lester Fleet

"Crazy Lester" was a burly dutchman, a master mechanic, and the owner of Cape Breton Diesel. His claim to fame was passing the rigorous Rolls Royce certification courses but he usually worked on ferries, generating stations, and large commercial fishing vessels.

One very cold day in late October Lester was aboard the *Silver Sharon* for the last booze cruise of the season. A lot of drinking was going on. When one of Dad's friends tried to board the dingy nobody noticed it was half full of water. As soon as he stepped into the dingy it flipped over and threw him against the hull, and into the lake. When he didn't immediately resurface Crazy Lester jumped into the frigid water fully clothed, and emerged with the man. Both suffered hypothermia and were rushed home into bathtubs full of hot water.

My job was to fill the bathtubs and play bartender to keep both hydrated until they could recover. Soon they were both singing as loudly as they could and Dad told us that was a sure sign of recovery. I'll never forget trying to make my first traditional Scottish hot toddies for Crazy Lester as he lay shivering downstairs in the tub.

Later, Dad worked a deal with Lester to maintain the *Silver Sharon* free of charge in return for using it six weeks in the summer. Dad was working in England for six months out of the year, so it worked well for both of them.

One day in 1983 Crazy Lester dropped his crew in Baddeck around midnight after a hard night of partying. He was drunk and alone at the wheel of the *Silver Sharon* when he went down into the aft cabin to use the head. Surprise! The water was nearly up to his waist. When he realized the boat was sinking he jumped in the lifeboat and rowed for shore as the *Silver Sharon* sank to the bottom. There were no lights along the shore so he roamed around for hours before he found a road and eventually got a ride home.

The Silver Sharon

The insurer, Lloyds of London, asked where the boat was but Lester couldn't remember. They needed to find it but Lester didn't have a clue where it went down. Luckily the wind and waves pushed the sunken hull nearer to shore so the mast could be seen sticking up out of the water. The Lloyd's investigator spotted the main mast and called for a barge to recover the boat.

Meanwhile, this was an illegal lobster trapping area. A legal lobster license from the Nova Scotia Department of Fisheries was extremely expensive so Cape Breton lobster poachers covertly set traps illegally. They tied a rope from the trap to a piece of log that floated just a few feet below the surface. The submerged float greatly reduced the chance of it being discovered and the poachers recovered the traps at night with a grappling hook.

Lester had driven over a submerged float and the rope tangled around the propeller. The propeller reeled the rope around the shaft until the float wedged tightly against the hull and the rope snapped. The spinning propeller shaft acted like a winch that created so much side tension that it bent the main shaft slightly before the rope broke. The bent shaft shook so violently it damaged the waterproof seals that prevented water from reaching the engine room. That's about when Lester went down to the head and discovered waist-deep water.

Eventually the seals were destroyed and salt water poured in until she sank. Dad was furious and forced Lester to pay the insurance deductible. In return, Dad signed the salvage rights over to Lester who had it transported to an area behind his house. He thought he would restore the *Sharon*, but salt water had taken its toll and his neighbours made him cover it up. Eventually Lester did fix it up but the salt water had destroyed the once-beautiful woodwork.

The Silver Sharon after her final voyage

Chapter THREE

Replacing the *Silver Sharon* & the Bacardi Cup

Searching to Replace the Silver Sharon

I came home for a visit from the Airforce and was shown pictures and specifications for several candidates to replace the *Silver Sharon*. One finalist stood out from the rest. It was a beautiful steel hulled motorsailer called the *Barralong*. This sleek 55-foot, custom yacht was commissioned by Mr. James Carr from Australia and built by the world-famous shipyard, Van Dam Nordia in 1972. Van Dam Nordia in Aalsmeer, Holland was founded in 1600 and had been building custom yachts since 1851. *Barralong* was my overwhelming first choice and I'd like to think I influenced the final decision.

History of the Barralong Name

We often wondered why Mr. Carr chose to name his vessel the *Barralong*. Perhaps he was related to someone saved by the famous WW I ship of the same name. We discovered that the original *Barralong* was a "three island" tramp steamer built in 1901 by Armstrong & Whitworth. She was requisitioned by the Royal Navy in 1914 as a supply ship but in early 1915 she became a decoy ship. Decoy ships, called Q ships, were disguised to look like harmless civilian freighters. They secretly carried concealed naval guns.

In May 1915, the RMS *Lusitania* was torpedoed by a German submarine and the *Barralong* responded, but arrived too late. After the *Lusitania* sank, the *Barralong* was ordered to attract and lure German U-boats to capture or destroy them. Her commander was visited by two officers of the Admiralty's secret service who told him, "This *Lusitania* business is shocking. Unofficially, we are telling you, take no prisoners from U-boats."

In August 1915 the *Barralong* responded to an SOS call from the passenger liner SS *Arabic* which was under attack by a U-boat. A nearby ship, the *Dunsley*, had also been torpedoed. The *Barralong* rushed to the scene but found nothing—due to a position error in the SOS call. Meantime both ships sank.

Later the same day, further messages were received from the cargo ship *Nicosian*: *Captured by enemy submarine. Crew ready to leave.* It was followed by the last message, *Help, help, for God's sake, help.* The *Nicosian* was coming from the USA with a cargo of cotton, timber, tinned meat, and 750 mules for the British Army.

German U-27 was still firing on the *Nicosian* when the *Barralong* appeared on the scene, flying the ensign of the United States as a false flag. When she was half a mile away, *Barralong* ran up a signal flag indicating she was going to rescue *Nicosian*'s crew. The U boat commander acknowledged the signal and ordered his men to cease firing. The *Barralong* sank U-27 and everyone escaping from the sinking submarine was shot by *Barralong*'s crew.

The Q ship Barralong in 1915

The following month, U-41 was in the process of sinking the SS Urbino when a similar event occurred. The *Barralong* arrived on the scene and unleashed on the submarine until it sank. The merchant fleet celebrated but Germans described the incident as a war crime because the *Barralong* was allegedly flying an American flag.

We may never know the underlying reasons why Mr. Carr chose the name *Barralong*. Dad liked it because his friends jokingly pronounced the name using two syllables and called it bringing the "bar along." This moniker was especially fitting because at the time Dad was the Chairman of Glenora Distillers, the maker of Kenloch scotch and Smugglers Cove rum.

There is an ancient maritime superstition that bad luck will befall any sailor who changes the original name of a ship. Dad explained that the bad luck could supposedly be averted if the original nameplates were removed and placed in the bilge, but it was unwise to tempt fate.

Little was known about Mr. Carr or his family after he sold the *Barralong* to the Gerber people, best known as the makers of baby foods. The Gerber family based her in Athens, although her ship's Port of Registry was Peterborough, Canada. This was an added selling feature for our

The Glenora Distillery, circa 1992

Stott family because presumably we wouldn't have to pay import duty. The *Barralong* was oceangoing, proven, and had twin diesel engines within a tough steel hull built to handle the punishment of the North Atlantic. I told him, "Dad, this purchase should set you up for retirement so don't be looking back in three years wishing you had chosen the *Barralong*." Dad completed the purchase in 1985 and had it delivered from Majorca, Spain back to Nova Scotia. That caused an incident because the delivery crew ran out of fuel due to lack of wind and had to call the Canadian Coast Guard to be towed into Nova Scotia.

The Boathouse

Wouldn't it be great if we could store the Barralong at home for the winter? To do that, we thought a boathouse was in order. But to get that done through regular channels would take months, if not years, to get sign-offs, permits, and permissions.

In 1983 the Canadian Parliament passed legislation to create Canada Ports Corporation to administer Canada's seaports. Dad had been newly appointed as vice chairman of Ports Canada, so he invited the board of directors and some senior staff to a meeting at our waterfront home. Dad threw a huge lobster feast flowing with local whiskey, live Scottish entertainment, and lots of rum.

After dinner, informal conversations got started with leading maritime engineers. The brainstorming resulted in the concept and design of the boathouse. In Dad's typical fashion, he got done in an afternoon what the government couldn't do in a month.

The boathouse was built at the end of a 300-foot pier and was specifically designed to dry-dock a 25-ton vessel by lifting it out of the water for winter storage. In 1985 Parks Canada updated the entrances to the

The Highgate House property showing the pond and boathouse in Islandview, Cape Breton, Nova Scotia, Canada

St. Peters Canal and replaced the original twelve-by-twelve creosote timbers with new concrete and steel. Environmental laws at the time prohibited maritime construction with new creosote timbers but the existing timbers at the canal had already been grandfathered in and authorized for use on the Bras d'Or Lake.

Dad purchased many of these massive timbers to create a solid foundation for the boathouse. A pile driver pounded each 40-foot timber approximately twenty-five feet into the bottom of the pond and then the tops were trimmed off about four feet above the water so they were all level.

Each vertical timber was bolted together using horizontal steel I-beams designed to distribute the weight when lifting a vessel out of the water.

The Barralong safely secured inside the Boathouse

A look inside the boathouse

The water inside was seven feet deep and the peak of the roof featured a long slot about 18-inches wide that could be opened or closed to allow the masts of a sailing vessel to protrude through. Two 250-gallon diesel fuel tanks were installed so that fuel was always available without having to travel to a marina.

The boathouse was surrounded by hills on three sides which provided additional protection from storms and high winds.

The Bras d'Or Lake was actually a tidal saltwater inland sea. The pond was fed by several freshwater mountain streams. One of them was aimed directly at the boathouse. This contrast between docking in fresh water and operating in salt water provided the best of both worlds. Neither freshwater growth nor saltwater barnacles could remain on the hull, so it stayed remarkably clean year-round.

The Bacardi Cup Sailing Race

During my basic training in the Royal Canadian Air Force (RCAF), new pilots had to list the athletic activities they participated in to stay fit. The concept was important for military insurance coverage and to ensure trainees no longer participated in prohibited activities like competitive motocross or parachute jumping. Our drill sergeant stressed the importance of listing all activities, even if done seasonally or infrequently. I included competitive sailing on my list as I'd crewed on the *Barralong* during the first Bacardi Cup races.

The Bacardi Cup concept was founded when Dad and a bunch of friends got together over a few drinks to organize a friendly sailing competition. The idea took off and by the late 1980s it became a highlight of the summer boating season. The Bacardi Cup ended with a huge Saturday night beach party followed by a Sunday race called the Schooner Classic. It was so popular, and so many people attended, they needed to sell tickets to defray the entertainment and beach cleanup costs.

Fast forward to 1990. While having a few drinks with my friends, Dave Kredl and Matt Evans, we discussed our mutual love of sailing. Dave was the most experienced, with a world-class sailing resume that included offshore races across the Atlantic from Canada to France. Our conversation settled on the decision to start the Royal Moose Jaw Yacht Club. It sounded pretty ridiculous because Moose Jaw was a dry prairie town in a landlocked province—but Dave had a plan.

The newly formed yacht club idea allowed us to complete an entrance application to represent Saskatchewan in the national military sailing competition in Victoria, BC. The winner represented the Canadian military at the World Finals in Argentina. Luckily, it didn't matter that we were in the RCAF and not the Navy because we were still selected. We

Glenn Stott, RCAF Pilot graduation, presented with the Base Commander's Trophy, 1985

were happy but not overly surprised because we were the only entry from the province of Saskatchewan. To add to our excitement, the RCAF financed the entire trip to the Victoria competition.

Our team faced stiff competition from the Navy crews but thanks to the extraordinary leadership of Skipper Kredl we made it into the top three. We didn't win, but the experience became a natural lead-in to further competitions in Nova Scotia.

The Bacardi Cup was considered a regional-level competition. This was especially important because military regulations allowed for sponsorship and encouragement if you competed at a regional level or higher. The regulations were likely intended to support high level hockey or basketball players but it applied to sailors too. For the rest of my career I was authorized time off with expenses to fly a military jet from Saskatchewan to compete in the Bacardi Cup in Sydney, Nova Scotia.

Those were the days prior to cell phones. When you left a military jet at Sydney Airport for a multiple overnight stay they parked you far from the terminal building. Then you had to unload and secure the aircraft before heading into the terminal to find a pay phone so you could call for a ride. Our home in Islandview was thirty-six miles from the airport so there was a considerable wait before being picked up.

In those days there was no way to alert my parents from the cockpit about my precise landing time so I found an innovative way. It was easy to do, perhaps crude, but very effective. Fifty miles from Sydney I descended from 35,000 feet in a steep dive over the lake near Islandview. Then, from the middle of the lake I would execute a hard left turn and aim for the house at high speed. Once directly over the house I would roll approximately ninety degrees of bank and pull six to seven Gs in full military thrust.

G-force is the term used to describe large acceleration forces in relation to the natural force of gravity. For example, if the natural force of the

Earth's gravity indicated you weighed 200 pounds, at seven Gs your body would weigh seven times 200, or 1,400 pounds. Positive g-force is the heavy feeling you experience at the bottom of a roller coaster ride. Negative G is the weightless feeling you experience going over the top of a roller coaster "hill." A military jet generates far greater g-forces than a roller coaster but you get the idea.

Just two, hard 360-degree turns at seven G over the living room was easily loud enough to alert the family of my presence, even if they were listening to music. Anyone who ever visited an airshow without earplugs can verify that this simple notification procedure was enough of an attention-getter to eliminate the need for a pay phone and long waits in the terminal.

Chapter FOUR

Passing of a Patriarch

The Death of Ian Gordon Stott, Sr.

Dad passed away unexpectedly following a car accident on August 6th, 1995. Brean and I not only suffered the sudden loss of our father but were also thrust into the role of co-executors for a complex estate.

The previous year when Dad asked me to be his co-executor, I agreed providing he would sit for a video interview to explain and confirm his wishes. Our family was fractured, with only sporadic contact over the decades with my mother Gloria, and siblings Kirk, Sheila, and Moira. We only found out that we had a half brother, Ian Jr., when I was in my twenties. Everybody got along and they were great people, but the family had been separated since the 1960s. The siblings were bequeathed generous sums, but I wanted Dad's final wishes to be clearly stated in his own words to prevent any later misinterpretations or hard feelings. Dad agreed, but life was busy and he never sat for the recording.

After the funeral services I positioned the *Barralong* a few hundred yards offshore in front of Highgate House. Mom, Brean, Kirk, Sheila, Moira, Ian Jr., Liz and Irene (Dad's cousin) stood on the stern with shot glasses of whiskey. The glasses were served on the same sterling silver tray Dad used to serve special guests. His favorite blend from the Glenora Distillery was still aging in the cask so we used Johnny Walker Blue, one of his favorites.

Irene was Dad's cousin from Scotland. They hadn't seen each other in over thirty years when she scheduled a visit on August 8th. Dad passed away on August 6th but we didn't have any contact information to notify Irene. All we had was her name and a flight number. Nobody knew what she looked like so she had to be greeted in the terminal with a sign so she would know who we were. It was absolutely devastating for Irene when she fully realized why Ian didn't show up to meet her at the airport.

The *Barralong*'s sound system played Canadian fiddler Lee Cremo's Tara Lynn's March to God. Lee was an extremely talented native musician and a family friend who lived in nearby Eskasoni. He was the Canadian fiddle champion and won Best Bow Arm in the World at the World Fiddling Championship in Nashville.

Previously, in 1993, Lee visited us at Highgate House and mentioned that he was considering a musical comeback. Discussions resulted in the formation of a new music company called Cremo Productions Ltd. I had recently retired from the Royal Canadian Air Force (RCAF) and worked diligently as Lee's vice president to help spearhead his comeback. Dad and I spent a lot of time with Lee in the studio creating his new CD called The Champion Returns. We started promoting his CD throughout theaters, nightclubs, and record stores in the Maritime Provinces.

The Champion Returns sold very well and was later selected by the Canadian government as a gift for attendees at the international

G7 summit in Halifax. Track one on the CD is a recording of my voice introducing Lee's return to the music industry.

As part of Dad's funeral ceremony, it was only fitting to hear one of Lee's fiddle tunes mixing with the natural sound of the wind and waves as we spread Dad's ashes over the Bras d'Or Lake.

As co-executors, Brean and I had to figure out what to do with the *Barralong*. Dad had purchased her through Stott Holdings Limited with the help of a shareholder's loan that was designated as "due director" in the event of his death. Stott Holdings owned the *Barralong* and several other real estate assets but did not have enough available cash to pay back the loan. During his semiretirement Dad operated a sailing school and charter operation, but without him as the captain, the company could no longer meet its charter commitments.

The *Barralong* was a luxury none of the individual family members could afford so it was decided she must be sold to meet other obligations. The title was free and clear but she had languished at the dock following Dad's death and was no longer in a marketable condition.

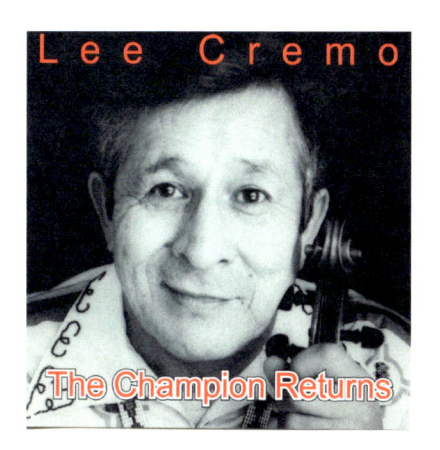

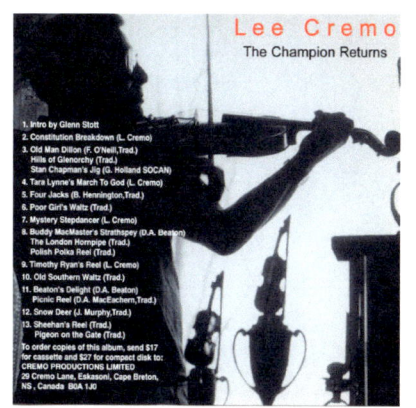

The Champion Returns CD artwork.

Chapter FIVE

Future of the *Barralong*

Preparation for Sale

The estate of Ian G. Stott received dozens of inquiries from prospective buyers looking to purchase the *Barralong*. Many were just curious and didn't have the knowledge or resources to seriously consider such a purchase. Nonetheless, Brean and I, as the co-executors of Ian's estate, decided that each inquiry would receive a faxed cover letter along with a detailed specification sheet. Serious buyers who requested additional details were mailed a packet of pictures and a video documentary giving a narrated tour of every corner of the boat. Most potential buyers preferred to fly to Florida, California, or Rhode Island so they could inspect multiple boats in a single trip. The video highlighted the *Barralong*'s unique features and was designed to spark enough interest to encourage traveling all the way to Cape Breton Island for a closer look.

Foreign buyers also needed to confirm the boat's condition before investing in a personal visit for inspection. To facilitate this, Universal Power Systems in Halifax was asked to visit the boathouse to conduct a marine survey. A marine survey is a detailed review designed to independently determine the current condition and seaworthiness of a maritime vessel. Qualified professional surveyors provided an unbiased, detailed synopsis regarding the vessel's current condition and the potential repairs required to operate an offshore vessel safely. The inspection also had to meet current Coast Guard regulations.

The survey revealed that one engine was no longer producing full power because a worn transmission cable prevented the gearbox from engaging fully. It also determined that both cooling systems were partially plugged, and the fuel tanks were contaminated. Replacing the transmission cable and overhauling the cooling systems were fairly routine, but the fuel issue was intriguing. Apparently, even if you used the proper additives, diesel fuel only had a shelf life of about two years. The air above the fuel in any enclosed tank contained moisture that condensed on the tank walls when cooled. The condensation formed water droplets that dripped down the walls into the fuel and then settled to the bottom because water was heavier than diesel fuel. This created the perfect environment for over twenty species of tiny microorganisms called "fuel bugs" that fed on the carbon, hydrogen, and dissolved oxygen in the fuel.

The fungal spores were carried by air and water that entered a tank through its ventilation system. Once the bugs were present in a fuel supply they could lay dormant and virtually undetected until conditions were right for rapid growth. Fuel that sat undisturbed in a tank was more susceptible to contamination than fuel that was routinely consumed and replenished. The bugs lived and reproduced in the water layer but fed on nutrients in the fuel. Some species looked like brown tapioca mixed with soft candy floss and reproduced so fast they quickly dominated any fuel system. They could double their numbers every twenty minutes and a single spore could produce over 260,000 cloned descendants in six hours.

Each spore lived for about forty-eight hours and as older fungi died, their bodies accumulated, forming a mat of black, brown, or green slime that ultimately floated upward into the fuel. When the wind and wave action rocked the boat at sea, the fuel sloshed around in the tank, stirring up the fuel bugs until they got sucked into the fuel lines. Their sheer mass quickly clogged the fuel filters and stopped the engines due to fuel starvation.

The bugs could be killed with specially formulated biocides, but they were concentrated, highly toxic, and expensive. We decided the most economical solution was to suck out the residual fuel with sump pumps and then open the fuel-tank inspection plates to remove any remaining sediment. A large fuel pump and five 45-gallon drums were rented to empty the tanks, but the pumps kept clogging and couldn't push the contaminated fuel up onto the dock and into the barrels.

The infection was so severe that when the tank inspection plates were removed, the bugs could be scooped out with a small gardening shovel. Then the tank had to be scraped to dislodge the thick layer of contamination that was stuck firmly to the walls. It was a hot, dirty, smelly job and I had to come up on deck often for fresh air to escape the stifling fumes from the engine room.

Barralong's ropes and sails were inspected, and most ropes were replaced due to damage from mildew, rot, and prolonged exposure to the elements. The ropes may have looked fine on the exterior, but time could reduce their strength until they failed at a critical time, usually just when you need them the most. A few freshwater line leaks in the engine room needed to be repaired and the furnace igniter replaced. Cosmetically, the hull and woodwork were in good shape but everything needed a new coat of paint and marine varnish to give her a fresh, revitalized look.

The Listing Agreement

Ian at the helm with Glenn near Northside East Bay in Cape Breton.

I approached several used boat dealerships in Eastern Canada but they had no experience with similar ocean-going, steel-hulled vessels. Yacht brokers outside Nova Scotia all required the boat to be relocated to a facility owned by them, as a condition of the listing. In addition to the cost of relocation, brokerage fees started with a ten percent sales commission based on the asking price, and not the final selling price. The seller had to pay the broker for labor and handling charges, maintenance fees, fuel for test drives, dry-docking inspection fees, and more. Boats of this type were predominately sold in Rhode Island, Massachusetts, Florida, and southern California. These locations were preferred because it was easy for prospective buyers to evaluate many similar yachts during a single visit.

The estate didn't want to incur the substantial expense of shipping the boat off to a broker in the U.S. so we decided to act as the broker ourselves. We could advertise and sell the boat directly in order to save the family many tens of thousands of dollars in brokerage, docking, and handling fees. The other problem was that if it didn't sell relatively quickly we would have to pay additional winterization and storage charges. We figured if a buyer couldn't be found within six months we always had the option of formally listing it with a broker.

The Prospective Buyer

Rich McClain was a gentleman in his early forties from Richmond, Virginia. He'd recently sold his financial business and dreamed of sailing around the world with his wife and two daughters. His well-reasoned plan was to start with a short shakedown cruise to the Caribbean in 1997, to discover any unforeseen issues, and then get them rectified in the United States. The next phase was to sail around the world with an extended stay in Tahiti for two years. During the voyage he would work part-time over the internet and the girls would be homeschooled.

It was evident Rich did his homework. He knew that he needed a heavy steel-hulled boat similar to a Choy Lee or a Van Dam like the *Barralong*. He also knew that Islandview, Cape Breton was far from the usual places to find one. A trip to Rhode Island or Florida allowed a potential buyer to see many ocean-going sailing vessels in a single trip so they were naturally reluctant to invest in an airline ticket to some remote area in Canada. Each morning Rich woke up and faxed a list of questions to Cape Breton, and each night I provided him with a list of answers. After several hundred questions by fax and a few telephone conversations, Rich decided that the *Barralong* was exactly what his family needed for their dream voyage.

He arrived on a Friday night and I took him to Smooth Herman's Bar and Grill. After dinner Rich returned to his hotel with two heavy binders packed with the *Barralong*'s technical information and operating instructions for the mechanical and navigation systems. Each manual was about four inches thick and Rich studied them diligently until he couldn't stay awake any longer. He caught a few hours of sleep and rushed down to the lobby for his eight a.m. pickup. He was wearing freshly dry-cleaned dress pants, dress shoes, and a white, short-sleeved shirt. He was definitely overdressed for someone who was going to spend the day crawling around the bilge to inspect the engine room, but at least he wasn't wearing a tie!

He declined my offer of a set of coveralls and jumped down into the engine room at eight forty-five a.m. At eleven-thirty a.m. we brought him a hot thermos of coffee and some crackers. He was filthy from all the grease and oil in the bilge and explained that he needed to be thorough. He told us he wanted to see and feel how she handled under sail and under power. It would take a few hours to call some of Dad's old crew to try and make that happen, so we started making calls to see who was available for a short cruise later that day.

At one o'clock Rich still hadn't finished his inspection and there was very little time until the crew arrived. He was still getting dressed when Roger and Marg LeBlanc showed up with Robin Campbell. Roger was a former branch manager for the Bank of Montreal before Dad wooed him away to become the comptroller for the Stott Timber hardwood lumber mill on Grand Lake Road. Roger's wife Marg was a bank teller with an incredible sense of humor. Robin Campbell was the Solicitor for the city of Sydney and had a bungalow across the lake at Ben Eoin. All three were longtime members of Dad's crew and knew the boat well.

As we loaded trays of food, alcohol, and soft drinks into the galley there was a strong breeze on the water and three-foot waves. Rich McClain was refreshed from his shower and the crew formally introduced him to the local sailing tradition of black rum and Coke®. He took his turn tending the main sail, then the genoa, then the mizzen. Rich said his goal was to experience every position on the boat in order to completely familiarize himself with it. Upon hearing this, the crew promptly sent him down to the galley to assume bartending duties.

After serving several rounds of dark rum McClain was amazed that we sailed about twenty miles and never saw another boat. In Virginia, he would have seen hundreds, if not thousands, of boats on a Saturday afternoon.

Of course, when the waves are three feet high and the winds are blowing at twenty knots, very few Cape Bretoners venture out on the lake, especially in a small power boat. The waves on the Bras d'Or lakes were short and choppy, making for a rough ride in any small fiberglass boat designed for calm waters. By nightfall Rich was thoroughly exhausted and desperately needed to catch another few hours of sleep before flying back to Virginia the next morning. When his wife picked him up at the airport she wondered what happened to him. His clothes were trashed. He was tired, hung over, and stank of diesel fuel and bilge water. She could hardly get a word in as he raved about the Cape Breton hospitality on the inland sea called the Bras d'Or Lake.

McClain promptly made an offer with the condition that the *Barralong* must be delivered to Virginia by December 1st so he could spend the winter preparing it for his Caribbean cruise. There was a sense that he was afraid of the North Atlantic and probably with good reason.

The Canadian North Atlantic is where the unsinkable RMS *Titanic* sank, and where the 1,000-foot-long Cunard cruise ship *Queen Elizabeth 2* was disabled by a massive rogue wave the previous year. Also in these waters, the massive oil rig Ocean Ranger perished with eighty-four people aboard due to damage from huge waves. The *Ocean Ranger* was the world's largest semi-submersible oil rig and had been certified to withstand 100-knot winds and 110-foot waves. It had operated without incident off the coast of Alaska, Ireland, and New Jersey before being moved to eastern Canada.

Pre-Delivery

McClain wanted us to arrange for a crew to deliver the boat to Virginia and he would pay for the new flares, charts, pumps, fire extinguishers, marina fees, and other delivery expenses. I estimated the cost of putting a crew together, paying for several weeks at sea along with their return airfare, and Rich accepted the deal. Accepting the deal would save our family the additional expenses of winterization and getting it ready for sale again the following spring.

Part of my pre-planning was a route study. This was an examination of potential emergency ports along the route in case of really bad weather. I was looking at water depth, fuel services, harbour lighting and shoals, operating hours, and marine services such as electronic or engine repair. So, when I looked at these things I was not only looking for a safe shelter, but a port which could offer anything we needed should we arrive cold, wet, hungry and, God forbid, with a hole in the hull. When I talk about route study, this is what I mean, Some people might see this as overkill, but having been a test pilot and flown search and rescue missions I knew firsthand how quickly things can go from hunky dorey to horrific.

In addition to the route study I had to contend with other worse-case scenarios. What if we had to conduct repairs at sea? We needed welding gear and a cutting torch. What if the marine radio malfunctioned? How would we restore communication? What if someone was swept overboard? We should have North Atlantic survival suits, personal flares and sea-dye markers, which is like a food coloring that stained the nearby water a fluorescent green color for up to an hour. It was designed so a swimmer could be more easily spotted by a rescue aircraft from as far as ten miles away. Sea-survival suits were designed to cover the entire body and leave only the face exposed. They were made of heavy neoprene to retain body heat and prevent hypothermia when immersed in frigid water. These worst-case scenarios had to be planned out in detail to inspire confidence in the crew and ensure their safety.

When I arrived on my pre-tour at the Atlantic Highlands Marina office, the operations manager acted like a bureaucrat who had no knowledge of the marine environment at all. She didn't know what the words "latitude" or "longitude" meant, and she certainly did not know the coordinates of the marina. She quipped, "You must be an engineer or something." To which I replied, "Why do you say that?" She was obviously annoyed by my questions. I explained it should not be unusual to ask these questions when you are embarking on a 1,000-mile journey and could arrive in the middle of the night when the office might be closed.

Requesting the latitude and longitude coordinates for the transient parking spots should have been a pretty reasonable request. A marina's radio frequency should be known long before arrival. If you saw an empty spot at a fairly large marina you couldn't know if the occupant just went out fishing for a few hours or if it was, in fact, available. The prudent thing was to plan ahead so there were no surprises and the office had your boat's name, captain's name, and your emergency contact numbers. It turned out she was a municipal employee for the town of Atlantic Highlands and had been tasked with operating the marina despite a complete lack of knowledge and experience in the industry.

The Delivery

The 1,334-mile journey to Norfolk, Virginia was sure to be an adventure of a lifetime. At a non-stop pace of seven knots in decent weather the trip would take a little more than eight days. Cruising twenty-four hours a day can be very tiring, not to mention rather boring. To make the trip a little more enticing a few stops were included along the way. The first stop was scheduled in Halifax for fresh provisions and to have dinner with friends. Then it was on to the picturesque islands of Nantucket and Martha's Vineyard along the coast of Massachusetts. From there we planned to cruise along the waterfront in Newport, Rhode Island to see the beautiful mansions built in the late 1800s. These included Marble House and the Italian Renaissance-style Vanderbilt estate called "The Breakers."

Marble House was constructed from exquisite Italian marble imported at a cost equivalent to $128 million U.S. dollars. The Breakers sat on a 13-acre estate overlooking the Atlantic Ocean and was widely acknowledged to be the grandest, most extravagant mansion in Newport. The Breakers was the signature symbol of the Gilded Age and featured 70 rooms, a 45-foot high Great Hall, gold-and-platinum-covered walls, and intricate panels depicting mythological beings. The next highlight was the notorious graveyard of ships along the narrow tidal strait named "Hell Gate," between the New York City boroughs of Manhattan and Queens running the span of Manhattan's 90th Street to 100th Street.

The competing tides from Long Island Sound and the Atlantic Ocean collided with the flow of the Harlem River to create a whirlpool and extremely strong currents. To make matters worse, the narrow channel was inundated with submerged rocks. The name was coined by Dutch fur trader and explorer, Adriaen Block in 1614, after he sailed his newly

The Manhattan waterfront abeam 48th Street, circa 2021

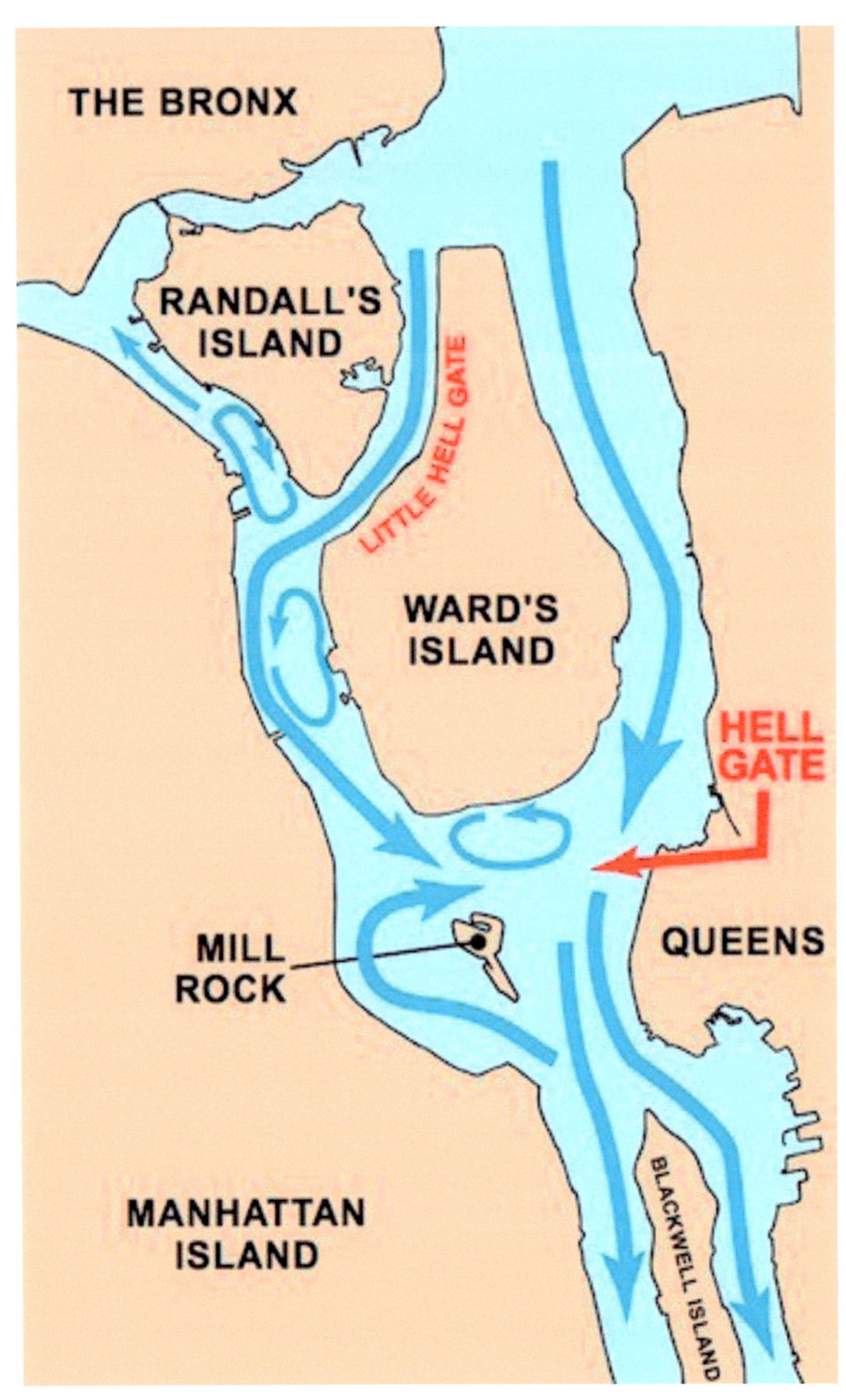

Water flow near Hell Gate.

constructed 45-foot, 16-ton ship through the dangerous passage to discover Long Island Sound.

By the late 19th century thousands of ships had run aground and hundreds more had sunk in the channel. Probably the most famous was the HMS Hussar, a 114-foot long, 28-gun, Mermaid-class frigate of the British Royal Navy. In 1780, the British Army owed a large amount of back pay to its soldiers, so the Hussar arrived in Manhattan bearing wages and seven American prisoners of war. She sank in Hell Gate with a cargo of 960,000 British pounds in gold, worth roughly $576 million today.

In 1851 the U.S. Army began blasting the submerged ledges and dangerous surface rocks within Hell Gate. This blasting continued for the next seventy years. At the time, the Hell Gate explosions were some of the world's most spectacular earthmoving projects. The largest Hell

Notice the Empire State Building dwarfed in the center of the photo, circa 2021

Gate explosion occurred in 1885 when, before an appreciative crowd of thousands, the nine-acre expanse of Flood Rock was blown away. Reports claimed the explosion could be felt sixty miles away.

The second leg of our trip through the East River featured magnificent views including the United Nations Headquarters Building.

Crew Selection

The family declared that I would serve as the captain for the delivery of the *Barralong* to Rich McClain. I had extensive captain experience on her and was a C-130 Hercules Search and Rescue Pilot, tactical pilot, jet instructor, and Chief Maintenance Test Pilot. I retired in 1995 as the Chief Instrument Check Pilot and Wing Operations Flight Commander for the 15th Wing of the Canadian Airforce. I also knew my navigation skills and ability to work calmly under adverse conditions would be tested in this role.

Lower Manhattan looking north from the Hudson River, circa 2021

Once the route had been determined, we had to select a crew. In addition to being competent and experienced, a good sailing crew needed to work well as a team. The most important qualification was for each crew member to have significant experience as a captain working with their own crew. A list of secondary skills was prepared and at least two people on the crew had to possess a mix of those skills: seamanship, sailing, navigation, radar and electronics, diesel engines, welding and repair, cooking, and bartending.

The first mate was Colin MacDonald, an electrician for Maritime Telegraph & Telephone. At six-foot-two, in his early 40s, Colin was an experienced mariner and familiar with Nova Scotia's rugged coastline. He was a well-known character at the Dobson Yacht Club and served as the first mate on the 45-foot Keoonik. The Keoonik was a heavily modified Cape Island style motor vessel owned by Roger "Chickie" Callaghan. Colin helped Chickie refit the Keoonik and built many unique systems for it.

Colin could appear rough around the edges but he was one of those guys who could hang by his feet in gale force winds and splice rope for you. He was also one of the finest cooks on the high seas. When you are tired and cold after being on deck there is nothing better than one of Colin's culinary feasts with all the trimmings.

Crewman Mark Ferris was a mechanic and local business owner who ran an auto repair shop. He had experience as a mechanic working on the *Barralong* for Dad and sailed with him on numerous occasions. Mark was a Mr. Fixit—a moderately experienced sailor but a great guy to have aboard. Mark was an adventurer, family man, and someone who knew how to get the job done while having a good time.

Crewman Terry Keating owned a construction business and was Mark's friend. He was a professional welder and a long-time boat owner who also could also repair just about anything.

Crewman Mike Sassco was a healthy, fit, young man in his mid-twenties. He was the youngest member of the crew and a sailor, racer, and marine navigator, but had little blue water experience. His family owned a J/24 in Islandview and he loved to race in the Bacardi Cup with his father Donnie. The *Barralong* was a larger and more complicated boat for him, but the basic principles were the same so he was eager for the challenge. Mike's family had a summer home next to the *Barralong*'s anchorage so he had often watched her under full sail. He had seen her many times from a distance and was intrigued by the opportunity for a long-range sailing adventure.

Islandview Departure

We planned to depart Islandview on Tuesday, October 1st, 1996 at ten a.m. in order to arrive in Halifax by three p.m. the next day. There was a new storm approaching the Eastern Shore but luckily it was not forecast to reach Halifax until after we were safely in port. Tuesday turned out to be a beautiful day and there wasn't a cloud in the sky. Unfortunately, problems installing the new bilge pump system delayed our departure by a few hours. Everything else was ready to go except for the pump motor, but it was a serious safety problem and the pump needed to be replaced before we started our journey.

There were a series of suction lines from the bilge pumps, one for each watertight compartment of the boat. A check valve in each suction line ensured that water could only flow only in one direction, but if it wasn't working properly, water could be pumped from one compartment into another instead of pumped overboard. Just as we finished fixing the bilge pump system we saw several cars driving toward the dock. We soon recognized that the cars belonged to family and friends. They were here to cheer us on and wish us "bon voyage."

We planned to exit the Bras d'Or Lake through the 2600-foot-long St. Peters Canal late that afternoon and reached the open ocean before nightfall. (The official name is Bras d'Or Lake, but locally we often called it the Bras d'Or Lakes.) Early French explorers named the lake Bras d'Or which meant *Arm of Gold* and likely referred to the sun's rays reflecting off the water.

For thousands of years, the Mi'kmaq Indians portaged their canoes through the woods across the narrow isthmus of St. Peters to reach the Atlantic Ocean. French fur trader Nicholas Denys established a proper "haul-over road" in 1650 and later, in 1854, the 100-foot-wide St. Peters Canal was built to formally connect the southwest corner of the Bras d'Or Lake to the Atlantic Ocean. The canal was needed because the water levels in the lake and the ocean can differ by up to five feet depending on tidal conditions.

We pulled away from the dock at twelve-fifty-five p.m.—it was a beautiful day and there wasn't a cloud in the sky. The winds were westerly at 15 knots so the waves were hitting us head on. With the winds and tides against us we were traveling at eight knots through the water but only six knots over the earth's surface. The new problem was that the St. Peters lock closed at five p.m. Six knots of forward speed equated to only 11 kilometers per hour which was twenty-five percent slower than planned. Instead of arriving at three-forty-five p.m. we'd now make it just in time.

Luckily, we arrived at the lock with time to spare. But unfortunately for us the lockkeeper was one of Canada's typical federal government employees. At four-fifty p.m. we confirmed that he was long gone and probably sitting at home already. We tried everything we could think of but there was no way to shame him into putting in a full day of work. We just had to resign ourselves to spending the night in St. Peters until the lockkeeper found the time to show up and grace us with his presence sometime next morning. In retrospect, it was rather naïve on our part to expect that any federal worker would still be on the jobsite fifteen minutes before quitting time.

The wind was now calm and the lake had become as flat as a mirror. The small village of St. Peters had a population of 2,634 so we walked up Main Street looking for an open restaurant. Nothing was open so Collin saved the day by cooking a roast chicken dinner in the galley. After dinner we decided to closely inspect the engine compartment before we went to bed. The boat hadn't been used in a while and it was the first time the engines had a prolonged workout. It was a good thing we checked because we found a loose injector line and two bad glow plugs on the port engine.

Each glow plug was shaped like a pencil with a heating element at the tip. When electricity ran through the tip it glowed like a toaster element to warm the engine and made it easier to start in cold weather. We replaced the glow plugs, closed up the engine compartment and got ready for bed. We all knew it was going to be a long day tomorrow.

Chapter SIX

St. Peter's to Halifax

Tricky Shoals

It was the morning of October 3rd and we left the dock the minute the lockkeeper showed up. It was an easy transit and by eight-fifty a.m. we negotiated the tricky shoals of the harbour exit to the Atlantic Ocean. Large kites could be seen in the distance, a sure sign of tuna fishermen. When a tuna grabbed a hook the kite would give a sharp tug downward, alerting the fishermen that he had caught one. We later learned that tuna fishermen can sell a single large fish for $15,000 US on the Japanese market. Not bad for a day's work!

As we cleared the harbour, the wave heights were steadily increasing and crashed against the semi-submerged rocks, sending spray high in the air. By lunchtime the waves grew to ten feet and the bow was punching its way through each wave. At one p.m. the wind was a steady 30-35 knots, the waves were 15-feet high, and the bow was slamming into each wave.

The gale force winds were directly in our faces so our forward speed was greatly reduced by the large waves pounding the bow. It seemed like we were making little forward progress as we passed abeam the town of Canso, which is the largest coastal town for over thirty miles. "Abeam" means on a line at right angles to a ship's length.

We were driving straight up the front of each wave and then vertically down the backside so there wasn't much horizontal headway. Crewman Mark Ferris was now deathly ill. He couldn't eat, he couldn't move, and the poor fellow was curled up on the settee in the wheelhouse, looking as pale as the whitecaps pounding us. Despite our attempts to revive him he refused to go up on deck for fresh air. Now, with waves crashing over the bow and occasionally pounding the helmsman in the chest it was too dangerous to go on deck. We abandoned the deck steering position, closed all the portholes, and battened down the hatches.

With the pounding we were taking we decided to cut the day short and spend the night in the small fishing village of Country Harbour. Country Harbour had a population of less than 1,000 people and was reportedly considered by the British settlers as the provincial capital and military base for Nova Scotia. Unfortunately, the first winter was extremely harsh and killed nearly all of the original settlers during their first year, so the new capital was ultimately situated in Halifax.

Country Harbour was only thirty-two miles away and Mark needed to get on dry land soon. He was strapped down so he wouldn't be thrown onto the floor but the heavy seas further reduced our forward speed. We soon realized that at this speed we couldn't make it to Country Harbour before dark. We decided to divert immediately to Port Felix which was the closest port and only eight miles away.

The narrow entrance to Port Felix was treacherous, with dozens of submerged rocks to negotiate before reaching the safety of the inner harbour. The path through the shoals was perpendicular to the wind, so the waves hit us broadside and pushed us sideways toward the rocks. To make matters worse, it was low tide. We were tired, soaking wet, and dusk approached rapidly.

At four-fifty-five p.m. we finally tied up to the wharf in Port Felix. Mark was kneeling, retching with his whole body, on the dock. It took a while before his color returned but soon he was up and walking again. He came back inside and told us that he might be hungry. So here we were, sitting together in the wheelhouse, safe and sound at the dock in Port Felix. It was dark now and we were thankful to have reached shelter before nightfall. Down below in the galley, Colin cooked a delicious roast beef with carrots, potatoes, and leftover chicken for the crew. The smell of home cooking gave us such a comforting feeling compared to the bruising we endured at sea.

Islandview through the St. Peters Canal to Port Felix

The sea still raged, and a loud, high-pitched hum came from the rigging. The rigging was a set of stainless-steel cables attached to the edge of the deck at one end, and to the top of the mast at the other. The cables were tightened, like those supporting a radio tower, and were designed to help stabilize the masts from sideways pressure generated by the sails. In these gale force winds the tensioned cables vibrated loudly like guitar strings, and could be heard everywhere on the boat. All night long the boats around us were slamming against the dock and the roar from the rigging cables made sleeping difficult.

We surveyed our situation at first light. Port Felix was an extremely small and remote fishing village with a population of only 310 people. It was named after Belgian priest Felix Van Blerk who settled there with the Acadians in the 1860s. The port was tucked well inland and private yachts rarely docked there, if ever. There was no store of any kind; no food, no milk, no cigarettes, no public amenities, nothing. The main public highway through town was desolate and we hadn't seen a car on it since we'd arrived.

The local fishing fleet was also in port waiting for the storm to pass. Their boats were called draggers because of the way they used heavy steel cables to drag their nets behind them. From the dock I could see the fishermen stretching their steel cables along the highway to inspect them for damage. The cables were thousands of feet in length and needed to be inspected for fraying, and to replace the fathom markings that wear out with heavy use. I saw another crew member greasing the ship and another repainting the wheelhouse.

Colin and I stopped to talk to some of the fishermen and then we walked toward the larger town of Canso. We knew we might have to walk most of the way because we hadn't seen a single car on the highway. A pickup truck left the dock and drove toward us. When the truck stopped to pick us up we realized it was one of the scallop dragger captains we talked to earlier.

We explained that we were hitchhiking to Canso to get some fresh food, beer, and to make some phone calls. In Canso, the captain stopped at the grocery store and waited for us outside. Then he took us to the liquor store, and then to a payphone so Colin could call his wife. On the way back to Port Felix we realized that he didn't need to stop in Canso at all, he must have just figured we needed a ride because there was hardly any traffic.

The skipper dropped us off and we invited him and his crew aboard for a drink. We soon discovered the reasons for the friendly rivalry between the commercial fishermen and yachtsmen. The fishermen call the yachtsmen "yellow booters" because of the trendy, expensive, bright yellow, Helly Hansen sailing boots typically worn by recreational sailors. By contrast, commercial fishermen wear the inexpensive black and red rubber boots you can find in any department store.

The dragger crew was fascinated during their tour of the *Barralong*. The skipper spent his entire life at sea but had never been aboard a boat used strictly for pleasure. He said it looked "clean and very fancy" compared to the working trawlers he was familiar with since childhood. He also said, "I've never tipped a glass with a yellow booter before." Before meeting us he said his perception of yellow booters was that they were a bunch of stuffed shirts who didn't know what they were doing. They seemed to just putter around aimlessly, constantly getting in the way of the hard-working people trying to make a living from the sea.

The next day, the winds were still so fierce that the fleet wasn't going anywhere. We had only traveled the first hundred miles of our 1,000-mile journey, but the storm raged on with gale-force winds and driving rain. The next few days were more of the same. Finally, in the wee hours of Saturday October 5th, the winds shifted 180 degrees and diminished, as the center of the low passed Port Felix. The local fishermen were getting ready to leave but we waited in the dark another twenty minutes before casting off because we wanted to negotiate the treacherous shoals of the inner harbour in daylight.

Port Felix to Halifax

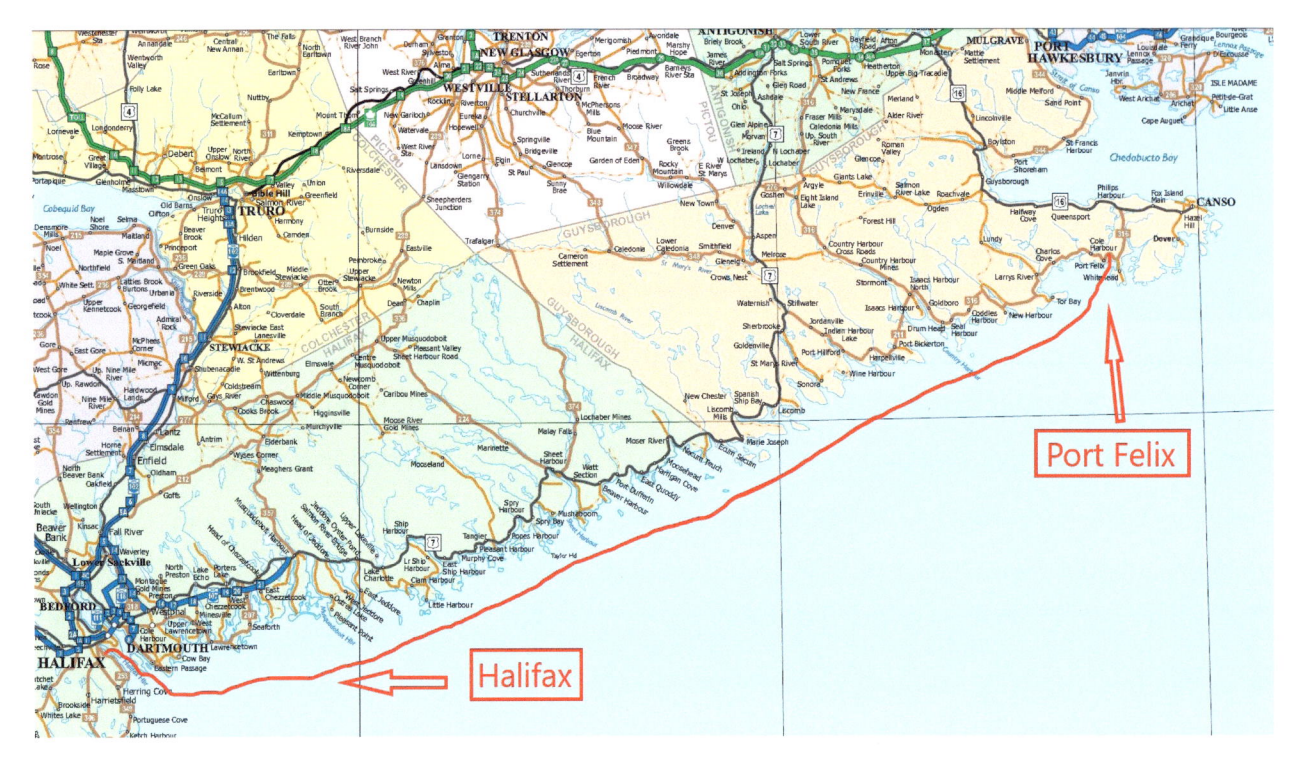

Port Felix to Halifax

We departed for Halifax at dawn. Halifax was an international seaport and the capital of Nova Scotia with a population of 400,000 people. The legendary nightlife in Halifax had earned the city a reputation as a party town and the crew desperately needed a break to relax and enjoy themselves. They were cramped inside the boat for most of our stay in Port Felix, so they were looking forward to arriving in Halifax before the nightclubs closed.

Mike Sassco was at the wheel on this bitterly cold Saturday night. It was not just cold because of the low temperature, it was that damp, biting cold that clawed through your clothing and chilled you to the bone. It was the kind of cold that penetrated no matter how warmly you were dressed or how many layers you wore.

As we approached the mouth of Halifax Harbour at eleven-thirty p.m. we saw Hartlen Point in the distance. It looked like we'd arrive in port just before one a.m. Last week we'd spoken to the Maritime Museum on the Halifax waterfront and arranged to dock there for a day or two. The Museum wharf was supervised, well illuminated, and very close to downtown Halifax, so we were pleasantly surprised that there would be no docking charges for our visit.

The crew was pleased to be heading into Halifax. The high winds and heavy seas had taken a toll, and our 18-hour cruising time to Halifax made Mark Ferris seasick again. We didn't have to tie him down this time but he couldn't help out the way he usually did. For the last ten hours he sat in the wheelhouse in an attempt to disconnect himself from the swirling ocean surrounding us.

Mark's friend Terry wasn't feeling great either, and both were separately determining whether they could continue this adventure beyond Halifax. Neither wanted to be thought of as the wimp who couldn't take it, but neither wanted to be back on the North Atlantic in October. Finally, we tied up at the museum wharf. The casino and nightclubs were still open but the crew was cold and exhausted. Everybody assumed they wanted to party but the lure of the sleeping bag was stronger, so within an hour of our arrival everybody was fast asleep.

It was Sunday morning and we were safely docked in Halifax. The plan was to top up the fuel and water tanks, mount a GPS antenna outside on deck, check the weather, and plan for our departure next morning. It was still cold, windy, and the forecast showed another storm was brewing. A closer examination of the weather showed that another delay was likely if we couldn't leave tomorrow. Colin was going to run out of vacation time. He took his normal two-week vacation to come on the trip and had only a week left to complete the remaining three quarters of the voyage. He was ready, willing, and able to continue, but worried that I might have to divert to Rhode Island or somewhere in between so he could fly home to be back at work on time.

Mike, the youngest member of the crew, was frightened. He was an experienced sailor but limited to sailing with his father and twin brother during those beautiful summer days on the Bras d'Or lakes. When I interviewed him before the trip he said he was occasionally nervous as a young boy when the waves were taller than he was, but he hadn't felt uncomfortable on the water for many years. This was his first time on the open ocean and his first North Atlantic storm. By the time we reached Halifax he was deeply terrified and realized that this voyage had dished out a little too much adventure. He sheepishly explained that he, too, was unable to continue.

That left just Colin and me. We didn't know exactly what additional challenges would face us during the rest of the voyage, but we were seasoned captains and knew it would take at least four experienced people to safely reach Nantucket. Theoretically, each of us could work a 12-hour shift, but that never worked in practice. In heavy weather with large waves, you couldn't rely on an autopilot. Just steering the boat was a demanding, full-time job. That left no time to tune and monitor the radar, spread out and analyze the charts, navigate, maintain the ship's log, or make something to eat. If we diverted attention for an instant when waves were crashing over the bow, the boat could easily turn sideways into the waves.

Anytime the bow was not pointing directly into the waves there was a very real danger of capsizing. When you reached the top of a large wave, only the center portion of the hull was in the water. The bow and stern were momentarily hanging in midair while the center was perched high atop the peak of a cresting wave. This left very little of the keel in the water, so you were vulnerable to gusty winds blowing the boat over onto its side.

Colin and I both knew we would have to find at least two more crew members. Time was of the essence. He was still very enthusiastic but I was concerned that another bad-weather delay could prevent him from making the voyage. If the weather forced us into another remote fishing village like Port Felix, we might not be close enough to an airport for him to make it home on time.

The next day we both arrived at the same conclusion: It was best if the *Barralong* started the next leg with a completely new crew and no time limitations. Reluctantly, I thanked Colin very much for his efforts and bought him a ticket home to Sydney, Nova Scotia.

Halifax—Stuck in Port During "The Adventure of a Lifetime"

I was alone in Halifax and needed a new crew. Luckily, we had many friends in the area who could help find some experienced people. Paul Quinn, who everyone called Quincy, now worked in base operations at the Shearwater naval air base. Francois Cousineau, nicknamed Couz, flew Sea King helicopters and commanded a helicopter detachment on one of the Navy destroyers.

Bob Simmons, nicknamed Puppy, was another experienced naval aviator from Halifax. Puppy and I spent three months together on the jet instructors' course in 1989, and later were both flight instructors in Moose Jaw, Saskatchewan. Marvin "Marv" McAuley was also notified of the plan. Marv and I used to fly search and rescue missions together when we were stationed at 435 (T) Squadron in Edmonton. Marv was now the Flight Commander for 413 Squadron's C-130 Transport and Rescue squadron based in Greenwood, Nova Scotia, and he was instrumental in helping to develop the safety plan.

[Note: When I flew C-130s for 435 Squadron in Edmonton, I flew Transport (we called this strategic), Search and Rescue (we called it SAR) and Tactical Airlift (we called it TAL). I chose this squadron because it had all three roles whereas the other C-130 squadrons only had two roles. There was no aerial refueling role in 435 when I was there.]

Each prospective crew member had to be a boat owner, a captain, and have significant marine experience. They had to understand that this was not going to be a leisurely Sunday afternoon voyage and that only "hard core" mariners needed to apply.

In order to attract experienced candidates the trip was once again described as an "adventure of a lifetime." Many people live life just going through the motions of existing but not really "living." They get out of bed, shower, shave, work nine-to-five, come home, have supper, watch the game, go to sleep, get out of bed, shower, shave, work nine-to-five, and so on. This was something completely different from most people's typical routine. A voyage like this was a rare opportunity and one of life's true challenges. It was something exciting you could be be proud to tell your grandchildren. My friends spread the word and soon a few dozen potential crew members came to inquire about the *Barralong* adventure.

I knew full well they were interviewing me as much as I was interviewing them. Each person carefully inspected the boat's capability, the engines, the sailing gear, and the overall plan. Charts were laid out for each candidate in the wheelhouse while the routing, emergency equipment, and the predetermined contingency plans were explained. The survival suits and much of the rescue equipment was borrowed from military friends so the crew was very well equipped for any contingencies. As the route was briefed, a set of compulsory reporting times was established to check in with Quincy and Marv McAuley so they knew all was okay. Marv's C-130 pilots would also have the routing and would keep an eye and an ear out just in case.

After four days in port the new crew was ready to depart for Nantucket. They consisted of Gary Hoff, Sean Holland, and Gary's friend Suzanne Miller. Gary was a tactical navigator on a large Canadian Navy destroyer and Sean Holland flew Sea King helicopters for the Navy.

Shaun and Gary were both boat owners, experienced sailors, and racing skippers. Suzanne was a good sailor and racer in her own right but was the least experienced. She was selected because she was knowledgeable, fearless, eager to learn, had good sea legs, and was not prone to sea sickness. They were all complete strangers but were well known and highly recommended by friends Quincy, Couz, and Puppy Simmons. A strong recommendation from any one of these fine gentlemen was sufficient to secure a crew position.

Chapter SEVEN

Sails Set for Nantucket—Adventure on the High Seas

We left Halifax Harbour at seven thirty-five a.m. on October 10th, heading toward the mouth of the Atlantic. These guys really knew their stuff so we decided on a four-hour watch pattern: four hours on and four hours off, cruising twenty-four hours a day. I put Gary and Sean on the same crew, as the two of them together could handle pretty much anything that happened. They familiarized themselves with the boat fairly quickly and some of Gary's professional experience as a Navy navigator rubbed off on the rest of us. I went on rotation with Suzanne and put her on the wheel most of the time. She was very capable at the helm while I did the navigation and log keeping until she was comfortable with that too. This crew was very experienced in the North Atlantic so I could get a semi restful sleep knowing that the boat was in capable hands.

The wind was southeast at 15 knots as the barometric pressure fell. Initially it was fairly rough but the storm subsided enough to allow a decent cruise along the coast toward Yarmouth. After passing Negro

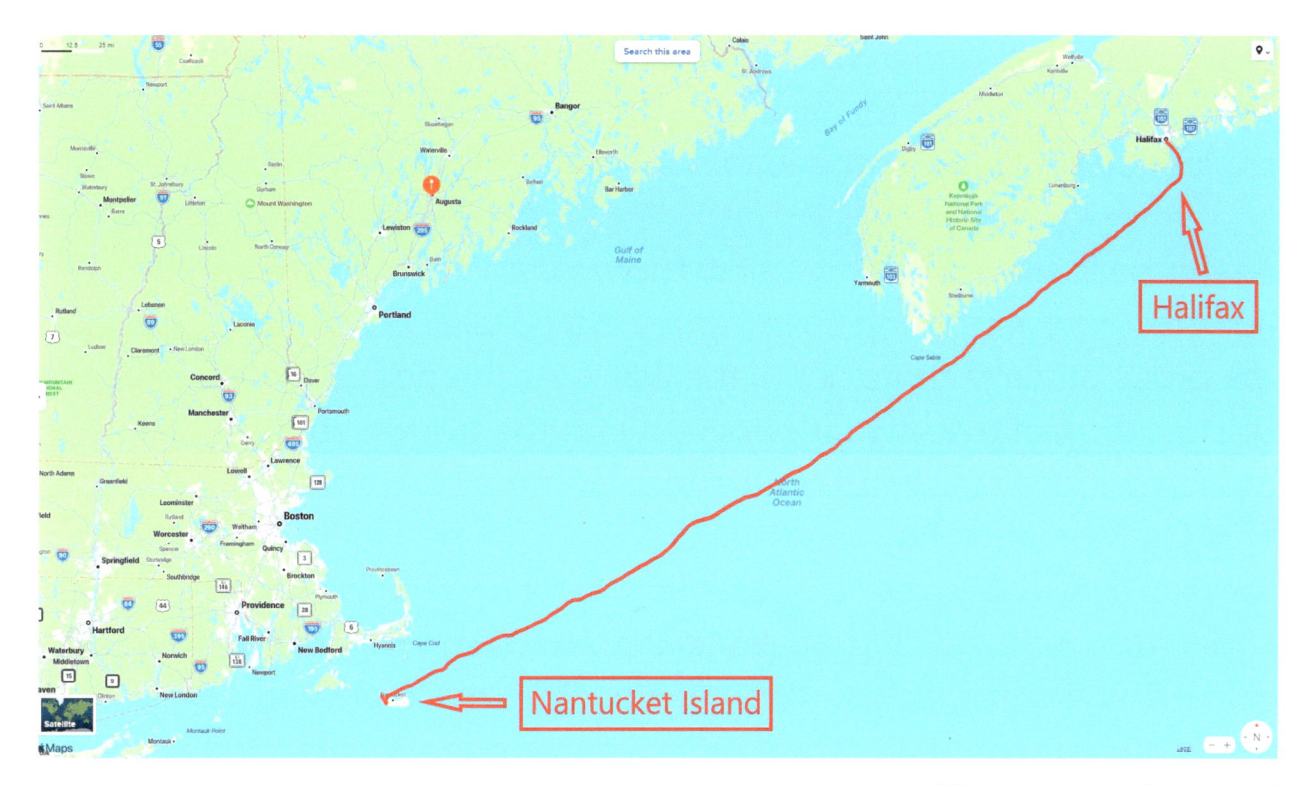

Halifax to Nantucket Island

Harbour and the southern tip of Nova Scotia we were in the open ocean and up to 120 miles from shore. We also crossed the shipping lanes of Saint John, the capital city of New Brunswick, which is known for its oil refineries and pulp mills.

We had to be careful at night, examining the ship's lights and our radar targets, to ensure we had adequate clearance from the bow and stern waves generated by these large ships. The stern wave behind a large supertanker cruising at full speed could easily capsize a small boat. At one point it looked like we were going to pass too closely behind the stern of a large supertanker so we had to make a slight course deviation. You never know exactly how big the stern wave will be and you can't take any chances in the pitch-black darkness of the open ocean. Luckily, we cut through the wake with hardly a bounce and headed toward Nantucket Sound and Martha's Vineyard.

Here the going got really rough; very, very, rough. In between my four hour watches I tried to get some sleep in the after cabin. I felt the propeller shafts churning under the floor of the cabin. Each time *Barralong* struggled to climb up the face of a wave, the props would dig in and the engines strained under the load.

As the boat clawed its way uphill there was a very deep rumble as the hull crested over the top, followed by a high-pitched whirring sound as the props partially came out of the water. As the boat accelerated down the backside of the wave it punched into the trough and the cycle was repeated as we struggled up the face of the next wave.

Larger waves swept over the top of the boat came past the wheelhouse and struck the brass ship's bell attached to the mizzen mast. On a twin-masted vessel the mizzen was the shorter mast located behind the towering main mast. Our mizzen mast was directly over the rear cabin and had a small sail used to help steady the boat in high winds. The mizzen sail was much smaller than the mainsail and worked sort of like a parachute. When the boat tried to rock back and forth the mizzen sail acted as an air brake to dampen the movement.

The ship's bell on the mizzen mast was used to notify the crew for lunch or signal an all-hands-on-deck situation. Every time a wave came over the bow it struck the bell and made a *ca-clang, ca-clang*. So there I was, lying in the after cabin listening to the winds howl through the rigging, the *ca-clang, ca-clang* of the ship's bell, and the incessant rumble and whirring of the props. Tropical Storm Josephine packed 60 mph winds and the atmospheric pressure was a very low 28.98 QNH.

We couldn't go outside because someone could be swept overboard even though everybody had a tether. There was the fear that unless it was absolutely necessary to go outside, someone could go overboard and get dragged twenty feet behind the boat on a tether. Another crew member would have to risk their life to bring them back in. It was just too dangerous, especially when some waves crashed over the top of the boat with enough force to kill—or at least slam you unconscious.

Down below deck wasn't much better. With the doors sealed, the portholes closed, and the vents turned around, there was a little bit of ventilation but not much. The Espar diesel-powered furnace suddenly quit and there was no heat. The furnace fresh-air intake was designed with an anti-siphon check valve to allow air but prevent water from entering the furnace. The hull was pounded so hard that a wave somehow blasted past the check valve and allowed salt water to flood the furnace. Without the furnace it was cold and clammy inside the steel hull, and the darned furnace refused to work again for the rest of the trip.

Condensation ran down the walls and everything was getting damp and soggy. Luckily there were several small portable propane heaters with circular reflectors to direct the heat. They were strapped to the floor because if one got tossed around the cabin it could set fire to whatever it came into contact with. There was a steel mesh screen over the flame but they still weren't very safe in a churning sea. There was also a concern about carbon monoxide fumes due to the poor ventilation. They were used sparingly under supervision, just long enough to take the chill off and dry the air a little before shutting them off. Shutting them down didn't go over very well with everybody but it was the safest thing to do at the time.

The waves pounded away and I was in the bunk when I heard the starboard engine quit. Actually, I don't think I heard the loss of engine noise as much as I felt the vibration change and heard reduced propeller noise. Groggy, I got to my feet as Gary burst into the cabin to report the loss of an engine. He suspected fuel starvation so I carefully climbed down into the engine room to find the problem.

It was tough enough to troubleshoot an engine when the one next to it produced full power, but was even tougher while a violent storm tossed the boat around. I needed to wedge myself in tightly before I could free one hand long enough to service the fuel system. The threat of being thrown into a whirling flywheel or scalded against an exhaust manifold was very real, and we couldn't afford any injuries out here. With great effort I drained the water separator, replaced the Racor fuel filter, and started to bleed the injectors.

I couldn't believe it! The port engine quit too, so now we needed to rely on what was left of the sails to fight the storm. I furiously bled air from the starboard engine's fuel injectors and within fifteen minutes we tried a restart. Ahh, success! That wonderful sound of a healthy engine! I repeated the entire process on the port engine and it, too, came back to life.

By now I was covered in diesel fuel and bilge water, and desperately needed some fresh air. I brought my tether on deck for a fresh-air break and discovered that if I braced my back against the wheelhouse, put one foot against a winch, and the other against the aft-cabin skylight, I wouldn't be thrown around.

I just sat there trying to relax when I spotted a small sparrow fighting the battering winds approximately twenty feet behind us. I figured she might be too frightened to come aboard so I yelled out, "Come on little birdie, you can make it, come on deck with me." Of course I didn't think for a minute she could understand me even if my voice could be heard through all the noise. I went back inside and told Gary and Sean about the fiercely determined little sparrow out there one hundred miles from land.

Sean nicknamed her Amelia, after the adventurer Amelia Earhart, and gave me some milk-soaked bread. I went back outside to find Amelia on deck. When offered the bread she warily gobbled it down and then rested within a few feet of the wheelhouse. She reminded me of a story in the Bible, when the dove returned to Noah's ark with an olive branch, proving that the rain had ended and the waters were receding.

Suzanne informed me our four hour "sleep" period was now over and we were back on duty. I felt better after the fresh air but still needed a shower and a change of clothes. The shower in the rear stateroom couldn't be used because the check valve for the floor drain stopped working. The forward shower was right at the bow, which pitched up and down thirty to forty feet in the large waves. Nobody had showered in days, and they convinced me to wait until the seas were calmer. By the end of our watch the salty mix of fuel and bilge water irritated my skin and drove me crazy. There was no way I could sleep like this.

I made my way cautiously toward the forward shower but couldn't wash myself properly. Each time I released a hand to use the liquid soap I was thrown violently against shower walls and the ceiling. It was an arduous task that felt like being worked over in a washing machine. I never used that shower up in the bow again during rough seas and was pretty sore from the experience. I must have looked in pretty rough shape because Sean said I looked like I'd barely made it through three rounds with Mike Tyson.

After a restful sleep I was startled awake. A quick glance at the clock confirmed that I had been sound asleep six full hours. After bolting out of bed and racing up to the wheelhouse, Gary told me to relax. He knew how tired I was and stayed up with Suzanne to help cover my watch. It was daylight but visibility was very poor. The winds had died down so the waves were much smaller.

I made a cup of hot coffee, and suddenly we heard the distinctive roar of a low-flying C-130 Hercules directly overhead. After flying hundreds of missions and living on a C-130 base in Edmonton, the sound was unmistakable to my ears. I ran out on deck, but after two passes they were gone, and we never did see the aircraft.

It must have been one of Marv McCauley's crew just letting us know we were not alone. What we did hear was a funny burbling sound near the bow. We were surrounded by dolphins, dozens of them, and they jumped and played in the waves created by our wake. Amelia was gone, she must have rested and eaten enough to resume whatever journey brought her to us. Best of luck little bird!

Nantucket to New Haven

We were all very tired when we finally docked in Nantucket at one thirty-five p.m. on October 12th. The boat was crusted with salt, the sails were ripped, the engines were limping, and the crew was stinking. Everybody needed a hot shower and a hot meal. After an early supper we walked along the wharf and met many of the local Nantucket skippers. They were a friendly bunch, and eagerly joined us for a drink and some sea stories. They all thought we were crazy to sail from northern Nova Scotia in October. We explained that our plan was to make some repairs in the morning, replenish our supplies, and then leave in the afternoon.

After breakfast Sean went to the marine supply store to buy some new engine filters. Gary went to the grocery store for fresh provisions. Suzanne was on deck mending the sails and I stayed aboard to study tides and charts for the next leg of the voyage. I closed our float plan with our friends in Canada, and had to check in with Rich McClain, the *Barralong*'s future owner, because we hadn't talked to him since Halifax. He had closely monitored the weather from his home in Virginia, and was understandably concerned for our safety, and especially the safety of his new boat.

Just as we were about to depart, a few of the Nantucket skippers we'd met yesterday requested permission to come aboard. They had grim looks on their faces and said they needed to talk to us. They asked whether we'd heard the latest marine forecast for Long Island Sound and informed us that it called for occasional 10-to-15-foot waves and winds gusting at twenty to thirty knots. We weren't familiar with the local area, so they told us that none of them would consider venturing out in such adverse conditions. They paused for a moment to let their advice sink in, and then waited for us to announce a delay in our departure.

They were shocked when we explained that this new forecast was the best weather we'd seen in several weeks so we were going to depart on schedule. In fact, we were looking forward to some better weather for a change. At one point the waves were eight to ten feet but the average height was around six feet.

Many tugboats towing barges transited the Long Island Sound, so we determined their course and speed to ensure we could safely steer around them. As boat traffic increased, we realized that our VHF radio didn't work. We carried a spare main radio and a portable hand-held radio too, luckily. We hooked up the spare radio only to discover it didn't work either. This was too much of a coincidence so we immediately suspected the antenna. The antenna was mounted on the top of the main mast some fifty feet above the water. It was just our luck that both radios used the same antenna, and the weather had damaged the antenna connection at the top of the mast.

Naturally, we tried the portable handheld. We'd tested the handheld before leaving Nova Scotia and it worked fine. Unfortunately the test was conducted outside on the deck. The range of a hand-held radio with its built-in antenna was very limited when trying to transmit from inside a steel hull. The steel superstructure absorbed much of a handheld's transmitting power so nobody could hear anything unless it was connected to a remote antenna outside. A working radio was absolutely essential at night on the busy New York waterways, but nobody wanted to stay outside on deck with the handheld.

We decided to divert to New Haven, Connecticut to install a new external antenna before transiting through the greater New York City area. The BoatU.S. marine supply store in New Haven was open until eight p.m. so we rushed to get there before it closed.

Chapter EIGHT

New Haven to New Jersey— Disaster Strikes with a Surprise Ending

The *Barralong* tied up at New Haven's Oyster Point Yacht Club in the early evening. The Oyster Point staff was very helpful considering the way we were dressed. We explained that we left northern Nova Scotia several weeks ago and persevered through several storms. We just needed to fix our radio and expected to be on our way later that night. As we stood in the entrance wearing our sea-going foul-weather gear and rubber boots, we saw a black-tie event going on in the formal dining room. The staff led us into a side room for bowls of hot chowder while we waited for a taxi to the marine supply store.

We returned to the *Barralong* a short time later and turned on the spreader lights to temporarily mount the new external antenna to the railing near the wheelhouse. Spreader lights were similar to a set of car headlights mounted high on the main mast to illuminate the deck below at night. We ran a new cable inside to the radio and realized we didn't have a soldering iron to prepare the coax connector. Every steel-

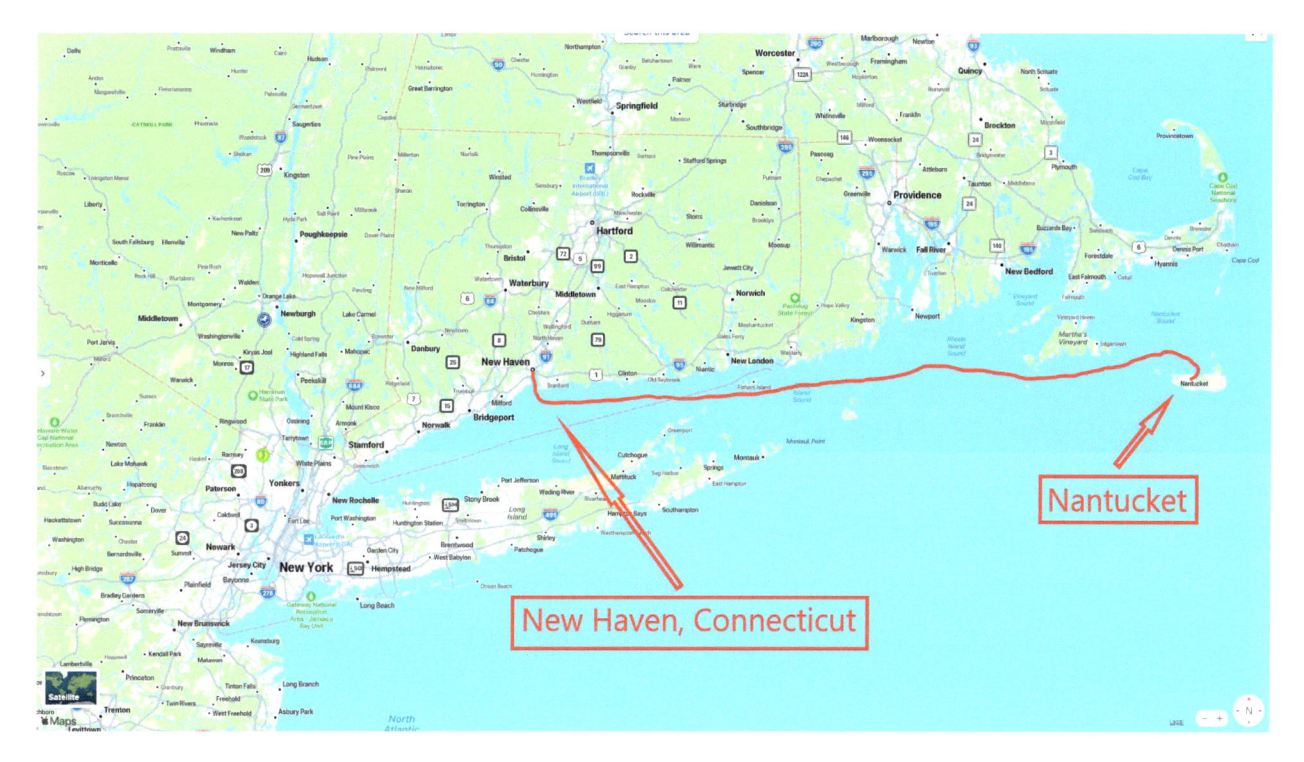

Nantucket Island to New Haven

boat owner has an oxyacetylene welding torch, so we put on welding gloves and heated a screwdriver tip until it glowed cherry red, and then soldered the connections with it.

We were so busy concentrating on the repairs that we didn't realize our super-bright oxyacetylene torch had attracted a crowd to the outside balcony of the yacht club. Word had spread like wildfire through the black-tie event about our voyage, and the battle-weary crew from Nova Scotia stopping by to repair their radios. The nasty winter weather of Canada's North Atlantic was legendary and they knew of the near-gale warnings that afternoon for the New Haven area.

They must have been intensely curious, because they sent down the maître d' with a tray of desserts and coffee liqueurs for us. He explained that the dining-room guests were amazed by our exploits and several had requested permission to meet with us. We didn't mind, so we gave them a tour of the boat and explained how we prepared for the adventure. They marveled at how everything was lashed down securely for heavy weather.

They were also amazed that we lost one of the forward anchors because waves pounding over the bow had snapped the bolts that secured it to the deck. The force of the bow plunging into the waves had also sheared off the stainless-steel bolts that fastened the decorative scrolling to each side of the bow. The scrolling panels were over four feet long and carved from wood to accentuate the *Barralong* nameplates.

I often wondered where the nameplates would wash up onshore, and who might find them. Would someone walking their dog along the shoreline see the battered nameplates and think there was a shipwreck? Would they wonder what might have happened to the crew? Were they involved in a heroic Coast Guard rescue, or did they perish at sea?

The decorative scrolling below the Barralong nameplates

New Haven, Connecticut to Atlantic Highlands, New Jersey

New Haven to Atlantic Highlands

As we cruised down the Long Island Sound later that night, the weather wasn't too bad. It was a dark night and we could see the lights of many boats mixed in with lights on the shorelines. All the lights blended into one another, so we used the radar to determine which lights belonged to ships and how far away from us they were. The lighting patterns told us which direction a ship was going and whether or not it was towing a barge. Long Island Sound was very busy at night so we had to be very careful. We felt much better with our temporary radio hooked up.

The other critical element was to pass through Hell Gate at slack tide. Hell Gate was a narrow strait in Manhattan's East River with strong tidal flows and hazardous rocks. Hundreds of ships sank transiting Hell Gate. In 1885, the Army Corps of Engineers used 300,000 pounds of explosives to blast away some of the dangerous rocks. That Hell Gate explosion was the largest planned man-made blast in history up until the atomic bomb.

Glenn warming up with a bowl of hot soup in front of the UN Building, circa 1996

We needed to make sure the tide was with us and not against us because we could be burning fuel for hours and not actually go anywhere. Thankfully, we breezed through Hell Gate and cruised down the East River to take in the sights. The weather was cool by New Jersey standards but by Nova Scotia standards it was warm and very pleasant. We were all on deck having soup because the weather was calm enough to cook hot meals again.

Previously, you couldn't attempt to cook a hot meal without being scalded by it. We took some pictures as we passed the UN building, then steamed toward the Statue of Liberty.

What an awesome feeling to cruise down the East River past iconic landmarks like the UN Headquarters and the Statue of Liberty. Then we went under the Verrazano Bridge and across the Raritan Bay to Atlantic Highlands. We finally arrived and were very excited that the difficult part of our journey was behind us.

The Atlantic Highlands Marina claimed they didn't know we were coming even though we notified them prior to departure and provided a revised estimate close to arrival. Months earlier I asked the lady at the Atlantic Highlands Marina where we would dock and asked for the latitude and longitude of the marina and the VHF frequency.

We arrived in Atlantic Highlands, New Jersey just before nightfall and naturally the office was closed. We tied up at the transient dock and taped a note to the office window, then proceeded to the Ramada Inn in Long Branch. Time to relax under a long hot shower and then wear clean clothes to a nice restaurant. The next day we returned to the marina to register properly and packed the car for the crew's trip back to Nova Scotia. They would also take back much of the survival and emergency gear we borrowed.

The Atlantic Highlands Marina in New Jersey

Disaster at the Marina, New Jersey

The next day we heard sporadic reports of a fast-moving storm approaching New Jersey. We returned to the marina and doubled up on the ropes securing the boat. Now there were a total of sixteen 5/8-inch braided dock lines; four on the bow, four spring lines on the port side, four on the starboard side, and four on the stern.

Later that evening, my wife Patti joined me, and we attended the occupational center's annual fund-raising dinner for handicapped adults. Just prior to the event I pulled up the marine forecast for the next few days. What I saw triggered my internal warning bells due to years of formal weather training and flying experience. My evaluation of the available weather data resulted in an assessment vastly different from the official forecasts. I was so concerned that we stopped by the marina on the way home to check on the boat. The office was closed, there was no pay phone, no emergency numbers, and no night watchman. It was already blowing pretty hard in the semi-sheltered marina and boats were pitching violently on the waves.

The *Barralong* was suspended between two docks so as not to crash up against either one, but the lines needed to be rechecked because it was only going to get worse. But a check would require a flying leap from the dock onto the deck which was pitching in the dark. Patti was wearing a formal dress and I was in a suit and tie, wearing slippery dress shoes, so the prognosis was not good. It was wet, rainy, and very windy so there was at least a fifty-fifty chance I might fall in.

The news hadn't reported anything yet but the VHF marine weather now agreed with my earlier analysis. I had to try. By the grace of God, another captain soon approached who also wanted to check on his boat. I agreed to help him if he would look out for me in case I fell in. I took a running jump onto the deck and landed okay. Then I checked the dock lines for chafing. I helped the other gentlemen do the same for his boat.

The next morning I went straight to the marina in daylight because I wasn't familiar with the local weather patterns. When I arrived in the Atlantic Highlands all hell had broken loose. There were boats smashed, sunk, and wrecked on the beach. Waves were crashing over the top of the docks. The storm rapidly intensified into a horrendous nor'easter and the governor declared a state of emergency.

The *Barralong* had been safely double-tied but many boats broke loose from their moorings and crashed into her. They got tangled up in the ropes securing the *Barralong* and eventually cut and chafed through all of the *Barralong*'s dock lines. She was at the mouth of the marina in one of the first transient slips so boats were still smashing up against her and sinking, but the steel hulled *Barralong* was still there.

It was chaos. I was worried there might be leaks onboard because the pounding waves were coming completely over the dock. As usual the marina management—also known as Miss Know Nothing—was less than useless. She didn't know where to get maintenance, pumps, or supplies and she didn't know anything other than how to pick up a telephone. In fact, that's giving her too much credit. She had my cell phone and emergency contact numbers but never alerted anyone about the massive devastation taking place in front of her. I decided to go aboard and shut off the sea cocks, just in case a fitting or valve failed below the waterline from all the pounding against the dock. I also wanted to ensure that *Barralong* wasn't taking on water.

It was sickening. Many boats had already sunk and several masts stuck up out of the water. It was a little scary to go on the dock because some waves were still breaching over the top of it. I could see that all dock lines securing the *Barralong* had been severed by jagged pieces of other boats and debris, so now it was loose and not tied to anything. There were dozens of broken pieces of other boats littering the deck and we later discovered from an insurance adjuster that 200 boats had either been smashed or sunk. Yet there was the *Barralong*, relatively intact and still afloat.

This was a big, concrete, steel-reinforced wharf and I didn't know how long the *Barralong*'s steel hull could take the punishment before it sank. The first instinct when faced with the ferocity of the sea was to run away and seek shelter. But something had to be done, and done quickly. I told Patti to take our GMC Jimmy to the automotive service station up the road and get as many old tires as she could stuff in the truck.

She came back with them, plus our friend Mike, so we took some tires and I ran out on the dock wearing my bright-orange, Mustang floater coat packed with marine survival gear. The full sea survival suits were already on the way back to Canada but if I was swept off the dock at least the Mustang coat would prevent drowning.

I jumped onto the *Barralong* with the tires and used the pieces of severed ropes lying around the deck to tie them along the side of the hull like a set of redneck fenders. At least now there were old tires cushioning the *Barralong* each time it slammed against the dock.

The marina lady was not happy. She had a loudspeaker and announced that nobody was allowed on the dock. Those poor people were just standing around listening to this bureaucratic dimwit telling them to stay calm as they watched their boats sink. Well, that wasn't going to happen to the *Barralong* on my watch. I closed the sea valves, checked the pumps, and shut everything down.

A police car arrived but the officers stayed in it at the dock entrance due to the pounding rain. It is still pretty windy so they probably were called to tell people the marina was now closed. If they wanted me to come in, they were going to have to come out and tell me. When the storm ended, just about every boat on that transient dock was smashed and sunk except for the *Barralong* and a tugboat from Louisiana.

The next day I was on deck trying to determine the damage. Our friend Steven was a property developer from Newark, and he came down to help assess the situation. Like Brean in Nova Scotia, Steven also ran a Kawneer architectural products dealership in northern New Jersey.

He employed a professional yacht captain and during the summer months kept his boat across from Manhattan at the Lincoln Harbor marina. Each year the captain brought it down to Florida for Steven to enjoy in the winter months. While we were standing there talking, Steven leaned on the railing to steady himself. The railings were damaged by the nor'easter so he tumbled overboard into the frigid water. Patti and I strained to lift him back aboard before he was crushed against the dock. He was freezing cold and quickly stripped down to dry himself off.

Patti's friend *Sharon* had arrived to help us, so *Sharon* dashed to her car and came back with her gym bag. An extremely embarrassed Steven put on her pink sweatpants and gym clothes in an effort to ward off hypothermia. He was embarrassed because his usual state was always well groomed and impeccably dressed. He didn't even drive himself, he got chauffeured around in a limousine.

Sharon rushed off with his clothes to the laundromat while we covered the chart table with the contents of his pockets so everything could dry out. He was lucky to be alive and was very self-conscious to have fallen in, but now he could barely even look at us while he sat in the wheelhouse wearing a woman's pink gym clothes.

By the time Steven was back in his own dry clothes, it was time to reopen the sea cocks, start both diesels, and plow through the wreckage toward a safer marina he helped secure for us on the Navesink River.

We later received a threatening letter from the commercial tugboat company that parked alongside us at Atlantic Highlands. We found out their reputation at the marina was poor because they were arrogant and projected a superior attitude toward all recreational boaters. They demanded everyone stay out of their way because they were a rough and tough tugboat crew. People avoided them. What a stark contrast to the friendly commercial fishermen back in Port Felix.

During the storm the waves slammed the tugboat and the *Barralong* into each other. The bow of the *Barralong* featured a beautiful pulpit which was a narrow walkway over the water at the very front of the boat. It projected a few feet forward and was covered by marine teak inlaid with white strips of holly. The pulpit's stainless-steel railings were soon bent and torn away by the tugboat's hull and witnesses feared the *Barralong* was doomed by the encounter. Everyone was shocked when the prognosis suddenly changed dramatically.

When the pulpit's decorative woodwork was stripped away it revealed the underlying steel structure. This consisted of a reinforced four-inch by four-inch steel post that supported the pulpit along with the masts and rigging. Astonished onlookers watched in shock as the post acted like a battering ram and took revenge on the tugboat. It smashed gaping holes right through the tugboat's hull and tore up everything it came into contact with.

Allegedly, the tugboat crew was furious and embarrassed that their big, bad tugboat was nearly destroyed by a close encounter with a "yellow booter's" prissy sailboat. Friends at the dock related the incident with glee and said they silently cheered because the locals hated the tugboat and its crew.

At the Navesink marina I discovered that many people didn't take their boats out at all, ever. We met one fellow on his 45-foot cruiser with very impressive navigation equipment. I asked him a few questions about his radar and the bow thrusters but he didn't seem to know what they were for, let alone how to use them. He didn't even know the type of engine or whether it was gas or diesel. *Perhaps*, I thought, *this wasn't even his boat, maybe he stole it.*

I said, "Surely you have taken this boat out at least a few times." He replied, "No never. I've never gone anywhere with it, never started it, I've never even untied it from the wharf." I was shocked and asked what he meant by never. He said, "Never, ever, ever." I said, "Well, you must have driven it here when you first bought it." He said, "No, no, are you crazy? I had it delivered and made them tie the knots at the wharf." He explained that at the end of each season he called the office and they came by with a crane and winterized it for him. The next year they put it back in the water, connected the shore power, and tied it to the dock. He had never turned the key on and never had any marine equipment powered up.

He admitted that he didn't like boating but enjoyed getting away from the noisy hustle of downtown Manhattan. None of this made any sense until he explained that his favorite summer passion was to sit near the waterfront in the sunshine with a good book. Apparently, this 45-foot cruiser was by far the cheapest waterfront cottage he could find anywhere near New York city to indulge his passion. Now it made perfect sense!

The Transfer

As we sailed into Seabright, New Jersey, the sky was deep blue and any traces of smog had been obliterated by the storm. The air was unusually crisp and clean. We'd made it! Finally! The cries of gulls welcomed us. Rich McClain met me at Woody's Ocean Grille in Seabright to have lunch and say farewell. He and his crew of three friends were going to motor back to Virginia through the Intracoastal Waterway.

Rich invited Patti and me to his home in Richmond to see the progress of the *Barralong* refit. The original equipment was twenty-five years old so he wanted a major refit to modernize the original systems and restore the vessel to a state-of-the-art global cruising standard. There was no insurance coverage for the freak storm that damaged so many boats at the marina, so we came to an agreement that satisfied both of us.

By September of 1997 the entire interior had been removed so a tough insulating coating could be applied to the hull and provide corrosion protection. The freshwater system and the 24-volt European electrical systems had been replaced by a new 12-volt system. Modern electronics and the latest navigation equipment were installed in preparation for the Caribbean cruise the following year. It seemed like an awful lot of work for a 25-year-old boat but it was worth it. Rich told us about fiberglass boats being torn open at sea by submerged containers and debris, so he wanted a rugged steel vessel.

Part of me felt sad to see the *Barralong* in Norfolk all torn apart with her innards exposed. I hoped her spirit remained intact through all the reconstruction, and that she wasn't upset with me for bringing her here. She was one hell of a boat and a big part of the Stott family in Nova Scotia. Looking back at the arduous delivery, it was almost like she never wanted to leave her comfortable home in Islandview, Cape Breton.

My last memory of her was standing on the dock in Seabright, NJ as she sailed out of sight. I was proud and sad at the same time. The *Barralong* had been an integral part of the Stott family and protected us for many years. Somehow, I knew she would be happy with her new family and watch over the McClain kids during their new global adventures. My only wish was that she was happy sailing the seas once again.

APPENDIX

*Pictures, Documents, and Memories
International Sail Training Race for the Ports
Canada World Cup 1984*

Glenn Stott, RCAF, informal graduation photo, 1985

Guide

International Sail Training
Race for the Ports Canada
World Cup 1984.

Sydney, Nova Scotia, Canada
to Liverpool, England
July 11 — August 3, 1984.

Ports Canada

Ports Canada World Cup 1984

Message from the Chairman of the Ports Canada International World Cup Event

Ian G. Stott

"Canadians from coast to coast are tremendously excited and proud to be hosting the "Tall Ships" this summer. We at Ports Canada are particularly delighted to have the opportunity to participate through the race of the "International Tall Ships" of the Sail Training Association. These vessels serve to instill the principles of international cooperation and seamanship excellence in their crews, made up of young men and women in training to take their place in the merchant ships of the world.

Ports Canada, being responsible for ensuring Canada maintains an efficient system of ports across the country, recognizes the vital role maritime trade plays in our economy and realizes the key function the world's merchant shipping plays in maintaining and expanding this key economic sector.

We wish all the participants in the Sydney, N.S. to Liverpool, England race for the Ports Canada World Cup the very best of luck in responding to this unique challenge."

Sincerely,

Ian G. Stott
Vice-Chairman of Ports Canada
Chairman of the Ports Canada
International World Cup Event

Ports Canada World Cup 1984

About the Cup itself

This magnificent original trophy standing approximately 1 meter high, was handcrafted by the world renowned Silversmith of Birks of Canada.

The Silver Cup, hand-fashioned in the shape of a quay bollard, depicts the Ports and Harbours of the World.

The handcrafted Canadian hardwood base is in the shape of a ship's capstan, a marine device traditionally manually operated to raise the ships anchor, depicting the trading ships of the world. The entire trophy with bollard and capstan joined, becomes officially "The Ports Canada World Cup". The original was designed by Ian G. Stott, Vice Chairman of Ports Canada.

The Ports Canada World Cup was a labour of love on the part of all who made her. It stands as fitting tribute to the tall ships, their crews, and their association with Canada's history.

Awarded biennially to the captains, officers, and crew of the winning vessels of any nation judged by their peers as those most exemplifying the courage, resourcefulness, and world class seamanship excellence demanded to achieve prime position in the sea lanes of the globe.

The Cup will be presented for the first time to the winners of the International Sail Training Race from Sydney, Nova Scotia to Liverpool England, July 11 – August 3, 1984. It will then be returned to Ports Canada in Ottawa where it will be on permanent exhibition at the Corporation's National Office. Every two years it will be competed for in the interests of international cooperation and goodwill, and as a reminder of Canada's deep involvement with the world maritime community.

Trophy and Awards for the Race for the Ports Canada World Cup 1984

The Ports Canada World Cup (A miniature of this cup will be presented to the Captains of the winning vessel in each class)

Gold medal struck by the Royal Canadian Mint to be presented to the Captains of the winning vessel in each class

Gold medal struck by the Royal Canadian Mint to be awarded to each member of the crew of the winning vessel in each class

Commemorative scroll to be presented to the Captain and Crew of each participating vessel

Financial Post Magazine article by Silver Donald Cameron

A TALL SHIPS TALE

The story of Stott, a canny Nova Scotian who launched an international race

BY SILVER DONALD CAMERON

PHOTOGRAPH BY ERIC HAYES

"I GOT LORD STRATHCONA ON THE phone," says Ian Stott, "and I said, 'I want you on the Orient Express that afternoon. Mon, it's no' for me, it's no' a matter o' selling aluminum windows! It's for the government, it's for Canada!'"

Ian Stott has no contempt for aluminum windows—he has made a tidy fortune out of them—but he was speaking in his newish role as vice-chairman of Ports Canada, which in 1983 succeeded the National Harbours Board. Ports Canada's 14 directors, all from the private sector, had already accomplished a major restructuring, resulting in a handsome profit on the corporation's first-year operations. Now, Stott was trying to raise its profile with the inception of the Ports Canada World Cup, a Tall Ships race, run this year from Sydney, N.S. to Liverpool, England, with replicas of the cup to be awarded in three classes. He wanted a crowd of celebrities to ensure that the world's media would be drawn to the August 3 presentations and celebrations in Liverpool. He wanted Lord Strathcona, for one.

He got Lord Strathcona. He also got Viscount Garnock, Sir Peter Gadsden and a pride of other British peers with Canadian connections. He got filmmakers, authors, shipping magnates, politicians, diplomats and hordes of paparazzi. He got the world's most luxurious train, the Royal Philharmonic Hall and much more.

Ian Stott has been, for most of the past 30 years, the president of Stott Aluminum Corp., operating from a warehouselike building on Welton Street in Sydney, N.S. It is a sound little business, generating about $2 million annually in sales, but it would represent no more than a burp if it were swallowed, say, by Canadian Pacific.

So why was Ian Stott able to put the arm on the international elite, manipulating cities, governments, navies and other immovable objects to serve the purposes of Ports Canada?

SHORT AND STOUT, WITH HOODED EYES that move easily from doleful repose to crinkled merriment or cold wariness, Stott sounds "like 98-percent bullshit," says another Sydney businessman. "Yet it's all true. He's pulled off amazing things."

He was born 55 years ago in Aberdeen, Scotland to a family rooted in fishing, farming and shipbuilding. But times were changing. Stott remembers his grandfather assembling the family and telling his sons that the wooden trawler was obsolete, and that all their farms would have to be mortgaged to start a steel shipyard. Stott's own father—"like all fathers," Stott smiles—decided that his sons should have something better, and informed Ian that he would become a lawyer. But World War II

The Financial Post Magazine/September 1, 1984   61

broke out, and Aberdeen's seamen enlisted "as they did for every war." Stott joined the navy at 14, was commissioned a sub-lieutenant before he was 16 and would cheerfully have stayed in the navy forever. But his father reached in and plucked him out. He was to be a lawyer.

During his navy years, Stott had visited Canada, including Sydney, which "didna impress me verra much." When his brother won a lottery, the two decided to emigrate—and since the boys were leaving, the parents elected to go along. When the dust settled, the parents were ensconced in Montreal and Stott himself was a student at the Blackstone School of Law in Chicago, working evenings in a restaurant.

One of the patrons noticed his accent, struck up a conversation and asked Stott what he was making. Twenty dollars a week, said Stott. The patron, Francis Foch MacDonald, said he knew a place where men with Stott's qualities were making $100 a day, and gave Stott the name of a man to see. Stott ignored it, but six months later, MacDonald returned. He was president of Weather Products Corp. of Warwick, R.I., and he insisted Stott try his hand at selling aluminum building products. By 1952, when he received his LL.B., Stott was a successful salesman. The next year, he became Weather Products' vice-president of international marketing. But he wanted to return to Canada, and when an opportunity arose to manage a Sherwin Williams paint outlet in Sydney, he took it for the experience, not expecting to stay long.

In Sydney, he articled with the legal firm of MacNeil & MacNeil while managing the paint operation. He also descried a local market for aluminum windows and contacted MacDonald. In 1953, he became vice-president of Weather Products Corp. of Canada. Six years later, he owned it. Meanwhile, he had started Stott Aluminum. He never did practise law.

"I thought one of the best markets for aluminum windows would be Scotland and England," he remembers, "so I went across with some of my windows. I told them that the windows could be manufactured there just as well as here, but because of our climate and experience, we were away ahead in design and installation." He landed some substantial contracts, negotiated a special deal with Air Canada and began flying planeloads of windows to Britain.

One of his customers was a prefab builder called Swift Homes—and a Swift home was chosen by *Woman* magazine for a national award. Its most desirable feature, said the magazine, was its double windows from Stott Aluminum Corp. of Sydney, N.S. At that point, Stott recalls, "the multinationals began to take notice."

Alcan was anxious to get into commercial and domestic products—and, while it was spending millions to crack the field, here was this fellow from Sydney exporting his windows and drawing all this publicity. Would he come to work for them? Yes, said Stott, provided that he had equity in the company. No, said Alcan, nobody but Alcan owns shares in Alcan subsidiaries; we want an employee. The negotiations were protracted and difficult, but by 1969, Stott had the right to buy 25 percent of Alcan Design Products Ltd., of which he became managing director and chief executive officer. He rose to chairman and CEO in 1979.

Stott Aluminum had a management contract, and in January 1970, Stott and his Cape Bretoners took over the 12,000-square-foot factory in Wellingborough, England. Over the next decade, Stott oversaw the expansion to five factories, 87 branches, 4,000 dealers, 5,000 direct and about 12,000 indirect employees.

In 1970, Stott took his Cape Bretoners to the 12,000-square-foot factory in England. It was glorious. In 10 years, Alcan Design Products was doing a £54-million annual business

It was glorious—Alcan Design Products was doing a £54-million annual business—and Stott was spending two weeks out of every five in England, where the company provided "a house, two cars and God knows what all else." Meanwhile, OPEC was giving Canadians the shivers, and the government had introduced the CHIP insulation program. Trucks on Sydney streets bore the legend "Stott Blown-In Insulation." Out by Sydney airport, a huge sign proclaimed "Stott Timber Corporation." Stott had real estate and other investments. He seemed to be everywhere.

The timber corporation was a brilliant idea that became Stott's most dramatic failure, and he is still tender about the subject. The idea sprang from the Cape Breton Development Corp., which uses six-by-six squared timbers called "chuck blocks" in its coal mines. Devco's chuck blocks were brought in from outside Cape Breton, but the island has plenty of hardwood: Why could they not be made locally?

Stott, says a Devco source, "took the concept, researched it thoroughly, got a comprehensive understanding of a complex sector of the economy in a remarkably short time and came back with a concept that had been modified and improved drastically. That sawmill was precedent-setting in many ways. It deserved to succeed."

"It was apparent to me," Stott explains, "that to make a chuck block you start with a tree. You need the heartwood. To get that, you cut things away. First, the bark. What can you do with bark? Can you burn it to make steam? Then, there are hardwood boards. Where can you sell the boards? Of course, you're generating mountains of sawdust. Can you make commercial or domestic fuel from that? Viability, you see, that's what you're after. Don't waste anything; use everything to make it viable."

Stott discovered British markets for hardwood boards and found Swiss machinery to extrude fireplace logs from hardwood sawdust. Holland had just banned softwood composition logs, so Stott contracted with Skelde Oil in Belgium for 1.5 million bundles of hardwood logs for Dutch markets. A chance conversation on an airliner led him to a World War II German munitions factory that had generated its electricity from wood. He examined the machinery and found that it was made in Leicester, England, where he ultimately bought a turbine. He even set up a hardwood-toy manufacturing operation to use the scraps and ends of lumber.

All bases were covered. Every part of the log was being used. The operation was viable. Stott Timber started up in 1980—and immediately received a double whammy that killed it stone-dead within a year. First, the business plan had assumed an interest rate of 11 percent—but the cost of money went to 23 percent. Second, Devco's coal miners went out on their first strike in more than 20 years and closed down the mines for three months. Stott's major customer was unable to honor its contract. Ian Stott "took a personal bath for over a million dollars. Enough to make you stop and think, eh?"

There are people in Sydney who think the failure of Stott Timber took some of the gimp out of Ian. "Fair comment," he nods, but he disagrees. It's true that he hunkered down and waited, but "that's just prudence. I don't know of *anything* that could have been started and been viable with an interest rate of 23 percent."

What Stott Timber shows, however, is Ian Stott's canny imagination at work. "He's a big thinker," says an associate. "He's one of a handful of Nova Scotia entrepreneurs who can be fairly described as having an international presence, a broad contact with significant players in the U.S., Europe and the United Kingdom, as well as in Canada. He's well respected by both the federal and provincial governments, and he has a reputation as one of the shrewdest and toughest negotiators in all of eastern Canada. He has a great many other interesting ideas, not all of which have been implemented because, I think, there are only so many hours in the day."

Stott himself says he has "always been a workhorse," and when he tired of commuting to England in 1981 and asked to be released from his contract five years early, it was predictable that his energies would seek other outlets. He'd long since become a patriotic Canadian and an ardent Cape Bretoner. "When you come to my home," he told me with a grin, "you'll see why." ▶

WHAT THEY DON'T TEACH YOU AT HARVARD BUSINESS SCHOOL...

"Mark McCormack's book is a revelation."
— Robert A. Anderson,
Chairman of Rockwell International

"Clear, concise and informative...like a good mentor, the book will be a valuable aid throughout your business career."
— Herbert J. Siegel,
President & CEO, Chris Craft Industries, Inc.

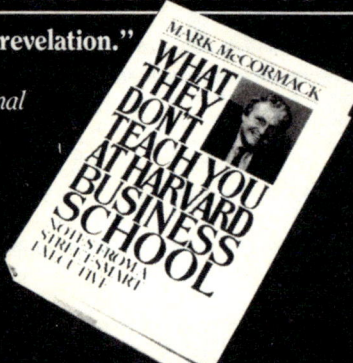

MARK H. McCORMACK DOES!

In 1960, Mark H. McCormack founded his business empire on a handshake and less than $1,000. Today, his International Management Group is a worldwide multimillion dollar enterprise. Now, Mark H. McCormack shares his techniques, knowledge and business wisdom in a book that's sure to become *the* business book of the 80's. NO CHARTS, NO GRAPHS, NO STATISTICS...just the best advice you'll ever get on how to become a successful "street smart" executive from one of the world's foremost practitioners.

A BANTAM HARDCOVER   NOW ON SALE $17.95

The Financial Post

PRESENTS

EXECUTIVE DAY

SEPTEMBER 5, 1984, THE WESTIN HOTEL, TORONTO

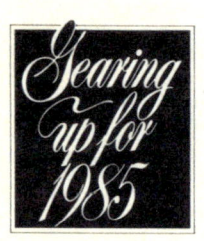

Gearing up for 1985

THE FINANCIAL POST is pleased to inaugurate Executive Day, an annual conference specifically arranged for senior management. Designed to simplify and improve budgeting and the planning process, this year's conference will have 'Gearing up for 1985' as its theme.

The conference will provide the kind of forecasts and business intelligence critical to executives managing divisional or subsidiary companies.

Expert information on interest rates, currencies, sector activities, international and domestic trade opportunities and political trends will be provided.

In addition, all registered delegates will receive The Financial Post's Quarterly Business Forecast for the year following the conference, beginning in October 1984. Subsequent publications will be mailed in December, March and June.

Plan now to register for Executive Day and establish realistic, attainable goals for 1985.

For more information contact: Rose Doyle, Financial Post Conferences, Maclean Hunter Building, 777 Bay Street, Toronto, Canada M5W 1A7 (416) 596-5678.

Financial Post CONFERENCES   in association with **AIR CANADA**

I DID. WHEN STOTT SAYS DINNER IS "informal," he and Elizabeth greet you at the door of their spacious modified A-frame in track suits. In a towering stone fireplace, square logs are burning—chuck blocks from the ill-fated sawmill. Stott growls a warm welcome and offers a bewildering choice of rums, Scotches and other firewaters.

The Stotts built Highgate House themselves. It was designed to be a summer home, but it's only 25 minutes from town, and they both love it. So why have two homes? Stott draws me over to the wall of windows at the end of the second-floor living room. In front of the house, lawns roll down across the road to stables, studio and boathouses, ending at a wharf jutting into a perfectly protected cove that is, in effect, Ian Stott's private harbor. Beyond the wharf is a mooring because, Stott explains, it pleases him to sit in his living room and look out at his 45-foot ketch, *Silver Sharon*, tossing her head at anchor.

Stott turned the full force of his marketing skills on British peers, governments, the Royal Navy, the BBC, embassies, breweries and the Orient Express

It occurred to him, he remarks, that it was nicer to have the boat at anchor than at the wharf, but it was a nuisance to have to walk down and row out to her. His solution was—predictably—unique: a Hovercraft. He spotted one on the way home from Halifax one time and made inquiries. Before he could buy it, his sons had picked it up and given it to him as a gift.

He hasn't used it much, though. It has to be doing about 60 miles per hour to steer, a trifle brisk for a dinghy. But, says Stott, lighting up with joy, you never saw anything like it clear snow from a driveway. Rrroarrr! Clear. Gone.

This, Stott says, is what really matters to him: the house, the boat, Elizabeth. It's all here—the whirlpool bath, the sauna, the well-stocked wine cellar, the superb cooking, the view, the 50 acres.

"I come out on this balcony on a summer morning," Stott declares, "and I take a deep breath of that air, and I'm ready to take on the world."

So after Stott Aluminum, Alcan UK and Stott Timber, he decided to relax and enjoy the bucolic air of Highgate House, yes? No. He felt like taking on the world, so that is just about what he did. In 1983, he retired as president of Stott Aluminum, turning it over to his son Brean, age 24. (His other son, Glenn, age 25, is a jet pilot stationed in Manitoba.) That same year, he was asked to join Ports Canada.

"I did it verra reluctantly," he concedes, but in short order, he had hurled himself into the job with his usual flair and energy. The new Ports Canada board took a money-losing operation and showed a $61-million profit in a year. "All we did," Stott says, "was apply simple things that anyone with any business sense would do. We got rid of a lot of people who weren't needed—I don't say they're not working for the government anymore, some of them are, but they're not on *our* payroll. We're committed to viability, and we made it a stripped-down, efficient organization.

"But you canna impress people by earning $61 million in government. They're used to such vast figures that you have to do something else to catch their attention." So Stott asked an official of the Sail Training Association, which coordinates Tall Ships events around the world, where the great vessels would refuel and take water after they left Quebec, before departing for Europe. Sydney, perhaps? Yes. And why don't you race across? Nothing to race for, said the STA man. Well, if there *were* something, would you race? Oh, yes.

Stott instantly proposed that Ports Canada contribute a trophy for a Tall Ships race from Sydney to Liverpool. The board agreed. Stott persuaded Birks to provide the Ports Canada World Cup at cost and talked the Royal Canadian Mint into producing suitable medals for winning crews.

The arrangements in England were to be handled by Ports Canada's public relations staff, but two of its senior men resigned simultaneously. Time was of the essence. With the board's blessing, Stott flew to England for 16 days—"Sixteen *long* days, mind you, with four telephones growing out of each ear." He drew on his contacts and turned the full force of his marketing skills on British peers, international businessmen, the municipal governments of Liverpool and Merseyside, the Royal Navy, the BBC, embassies, breweries and railroad owners. Like all good salesmen, he believes in what he is selling, and he can be almost irresistible. He came home with a sheaf of commitments.

> *We have saltwater ports, freshwater ports, big ones, small ones, warm ones, arctic ones: Stott wants to market that expertise to other countries*

The Sydney-Liverpool race inaugurated a permanent Canadian presence in the most stirring and prestigious of nautical events. Every two years, each time in a different hemisphere, the world's great sailing ships will race for the trophy bearing the name of Ports Canada. (This year's winners were the *Kruzenstern*, the *Swantje* and the *Flora*.)

Government PR people, it turned out, literally could not believe what Stott had done in two weeks. "I didn't realize I had a credibility problem," he reflects, but he learned much later that his report of what had been done seemed so unbelievable that the federal government, believing it would take six months to set up such an event, actually flew a man to England to check on Stott's truthfulness.

All of which seems to inaugurate a new public phase to Stott's career. As this is written, Ports Canada is staging a think tank in Winnipeg, considering its future. Stott believes that Canada has a unique experience in port development. We have saltwater ports, freshwater ports, big ones, small ones, warm ones, arctic ones and so on. Why can't that expertise be marketed? Why can't we contract for port development, government-to-government, and farm the work out to private Canadian firms? Unprecedented, yes, but "why can it no' be done?"

Most recently, Stott has been appointed to a Task Force on Deep Sea Shipping established by Transport Minister Lloyd Axworthy. Stott is well known to federal politicians Allan MacEachen and Gerald Regan, which may help explain the government's awareness of him. Stott thinks the task force may be very useful. Canada was once a major presence in shipping. Why can it no' be so again?

That is Stott's trademark, that canny imagination discerning opportunities away out on the horizon. And then that insistent question: Why can it no' be done? ∎

It takes energy to produce energy.

Energy to create improved oil sands technology so Canada's vast deposits can be better utilized.

Energy to increase heavy oil production...carry out conventional oil and gas exploration...improve refinery efficiency.

At Suncor we're making major commitments in all these areas. Because we know it takes that kind of energy for Canada to achieve energy self-sufficiency.

Suncor inc.
In search of the answers

License to cruise the waters of the United States

THE UNITED STATES OF AMERICA

U.S. Customs Service
Region I

LICENSE TO CRUISE IN THE WATERS OF THE UNITED STATES

TO: District Director of Customs

For a period of _1-YEAR_ from _10/14/96_ the
(date)

CANADIAN yacht _BARRALONX_
(flag)   (rig)   (named)

belonging to _GLENN STOTT III_
(name of owner)

of _HIGHGATE HOUSE EAST BAY N.S. CANADA_
(address)

shall be permitted to arrive at and depart from the United States and to cruise in the waters of the Customs collection district of _EAST COAST UNITED STATES_.
(name of district or districts)

without entering and clearing, without filing manifests and obtaining or delivering permits to proceed, and without the payment of entry and clearance fees, or fees for receiving manifests and granting permits to proceed, duty on tonnage, tonnage tax, or light money.

This license is granted subject to the condition that the yacht named herein shall not engage in trade or violate the laws of the United States, in any respect.

Upon arrival at each port or place in the United States, the master shall report the fact of arrival to the Customs Officer at the nearest Customhouse. Such report shall be made within 24 hours, exclusive of any day on which the Customhouse is not open for marine business.

ISSUED THIS _14th_ DAY OF _OCT_, 19_96_.

PLEASE SIGN HERE	SIGNATURE OF PORT DIRECTOR	PORT	DISTRICT
		Plymouth, Ma	

** WARNING **

FAILURE TO REPORT AT EACH PORT OR PLACE IN THE UNITED STATES MAY RESULT IN A PENALTY OR FOREITURE OF THE VESSEL.

I-RC-131
3/4/77

UNITED STATES CUSTOMS SERVICE
PORT OF NEW BEDFORD, MASS.
37N. 2nd. St.
NEW BEDFORD, MASS. 02740
(508) 994-5158

*SEE REVERSE SIDE FOR PHONE NUMBERS

Reference letter for First Mate Gary Hof

Stott Holdings Limited
P.O. BOX 45 · SYDNEY, N.S. B1P 6G9 · (902) 828-2765

To whom it may concern,

I had the pleasure of having Gary Hoff as my first mate aboard our yacht BARRALONG during an 8 day voyage from Halifax, Nova Scotia to Atlantic Highlands, New Jersey. We departed Halifax during the very challenging weather conditions of October and motor-sailed 24 hours a day for 8 days using a 4 hour watch rotation. We experienced gales for 4 of the 8 days, with winds gusting to 40 Knots and sea state 5.

Vessel	"BARRALONG" 55 foot Van Dam Cutter Ketch
Registration	Peterborough, Ontario, Canada #370129
Displacement	22.60 Tons
Power	Twin Volvo MD21 Diesels
Sail	Main, Mizzen, Yankee Staysail, ProFurl 150 Genoa
Routing	Halifax, NS direct Martha's Vineyard, MA Long Island Sound direct New Haven, CT, down the East River through Hell's Gate and Manhattan to New York Harbour, then down the coast to Atlantic Highlands, New Jersey

Gary's extensive marine background was immediately apparent and greatly assisted in helping my voyage run smoothly. He stood watch during very challenging weather conditions, mended seams, charted our progress, conducted enroute maintenance, and showed his ingenuity by soldering a VHF antenna connector using a propane torch and several pairs of vise grips as a heat sink.

We enjoyed having Gary aboard. I am confident in his knowledge and expertise, and feel he is capable of taking the BARRALONG himself. I strongly recommend him to anyone considering a similar voyage.

Glenn G. Stott

Sample of interest letter to purchase the *Barralong*

STARUCH ASSOCIATES
ARCHITECTS • PLANNERS • ENGINEERS • CONSULTANTS

M. HERBERT STARUCH, A.I.A., P.P.
- LIC.: NJ, NY, PA, DE, MD, VT, FL
- NCARB CERTIFIED

DAVID F. PLEWA

11 SOUTH GATEWAY
TOMS RIVER, N J 08753
TELEPHONE: (908) 341-9090
FAX: (908) 341-9030

July 8, 1996

Ian Stott Holding Limited of Highgate House
Att: Mr. Glenn Stott
Island View - RR#2
East Bay, Nova Scotia
Canada, B0A 1H0

Dear Glenn,

Enclosed please find a confirmed itinerary for myself and Joe Lombardi, the Surveyor. I shall arrive at the boat on Sunday, July 14, 1996, (PM). The surveyor shall arrive some time Wednesday, July 17, 1996. We shall survey the boat on July 17th and July 18, 1996. If the boat is not in the boat house, I would like a short sea trial. But, this can be done after survey.

To survey the boat, Joe requires the boat to be out of the water in the boat house to inspect shafts, props, bearings, and ultra sound the keel. He will also need access to the keel ballast which may require removal of some part of the floor to allow him to get to the ballast. Can you arrange for this access.

I am enclosing a proposed bill of sale subject to the survey. Tentatively, I would like to finalize purchase with Merck (Labs) Credit Union certified check for the balance June 30 +/- and leave August 1, 1996. However, I may finance part of the purchase price which could modify that schedule.

These long range plans are difficult to coordinate. I am relying on your participation in coordinating the mechanical, engines, and fuel tank and bilge access so there will be no delay in the transfer of ownership. Hope it all works smoothly. Look forward to meeting you and seeing this craft.

Thanking you in advance for your efforts.

Sincerely yours,

M. Herbert Staruch

For Mariners Only
Technical and Mechanical Details

Silver Sharon Training

Brean and I enjoyed sailing. During our late teens we wanted to take the boat out alone with our friends. Dad explained that we were too young to afford any repairs, so we had to demonstrate we were skilled enough to be responsible for it.

He devised a list of the individual skills Brean and I had to master before we could take the *Silver Sharon* out alone for a cruise with our friends.

Some of the performance objectives were;
- Marine weather forecasting and local phenomena
- Marine construction and seaworthiness
- Knots and practical seamanship
- Route planning and chartwork
- Refueling and provisioning
- Docking procedures
- Pre-start inspections
- Coastal navigation
- Radar tuning and interpretation
- Sailing
- Pollution prevention
- Lifesaving and man-overboard drills
- Emergency procedures and distress signals

On the day of my final test I entered the wheelhouse to find the front and side windows covered over with newspaper. Dad had covered the windows to simulate a fog bank and test my ability to navigate through the narrow channels between the "McPhee Islands" which was our local name for the Indian Islands near Eskasoni. I couldn't see outside so navigation was only possible using radar and a chart.

Once we safely cleared the islands, Dad removed the newspaper, shut down the engine, and said it was time to sail back to Highgate House. No problem, I thought. It turned into a big problem. Without an engine there was only one chance to thread through the narrow 15-foot-wide channel into the pond. If you missed the center of the channel while under sail, you would certainly run aground resulting in serious damage to the hull from waves and tides. If you judged it right and made it through the channel into the pond, there was very little wind. The pond had trees and hills on three sides blocking the wind, so you had to have enough momentum to coast a few hundred yards to reach the dock. Once close to the dock, you had to move fast enough to steer but not so fast that you couldn't stop at the dock.

Under sail, a boat needed to move fast enough to make water flow over the rudder to enable a turn. At very low speeds the rudder became totally ineffective, and you couldn't turn. The propeller was mounted directly in front of the rudder so the engine could push water past the rudder at slow speeds, if needed, artificially increasing its effectiveness. Docking under sail was especially tricky, but my young crew trained hard to master docking under adverse conditions. We were young and nimble, so the practice paid off. We passed the test!

Waterproof Seals

One of the main problems early marine designers overcame was how to run a propeller shaft from the engine room out through the hull to the underside of the boat. The propeller needed to be deep underwater to prevent cavitation, and the shaft had to spin freely. At the same time, water couldn't be allowed to enter through the shaft opening even though the propeller exerted tremendous force by pushing on the transmission when in forward gear. In reverse the prop tried to rip the shaft out of the boat as it pulled the boat's weight backwards.
The shaft fitted inside the bearing coupling with a light interference fit. A light interference fit meant it didn't slide onto the shaft at room

temperature. Even if you looked closely at the coupling and tried to push it onto the shaft, it looked like it wouldn't fit. That's because the outer diameter of the shaft was only 0.0005" smaller than the inner diameter of the coupling. That's less than the thickness of a human hair. That meant that the coupling would require some heating to expand it enough to slide over the shaft. Even with the heat it would take some light tapping for a proper fit to seal the water out.

G-force

The term "g-force" was often associated with aviation movies like Top Gun. The "g" referred to gravity but was really caused by acceleration. The force felt under acceleration was measured in multiples of gravity, or Gs. Picture a 200-pound person sitting on a bathroom scale mounted to a seat on a roller coaster. Before the ride started, the scale would read 200 pounds, which was the normal force of gravity or 1G. As the coaster sped over the top, that weightless feeling was called zero G, and the scale would read zero. When the coaster sped downhill and then rapidly changed direction to accelerate uphill, the body would feel very heavy. If the scale now registered 600 pounds, the 200-pound body was experiencing three times the force of gravity, or 3G.

G-force placed a lot of stress on the body and was extremely tiring. At 3G every part of your body weighed three times what it did normally. It took a lot more effort to raise the arms and the blood got heavy too. As the g-force drained heavy blood from your head down toward your feet the following phenomena ocurred: First, a reduction in oxygenated blood to the eyes caused grayout or tunnel vision. During grayout you could still think and hear, but it reduced your peripheral vision and color perception so everything looked gray. It took two to three seconds back at 1G to recover but if the excessive G persisted it caused a complete loss of eyesight, commonly called "blackout." The pilot was conscious and could hear, feel, and think, but couldn't see. Recovery time took two or three seconds after the g-force was released.

If the g-force was sustained, the next phenomena was a loss of consciousness. The pilot could not see, hear, or think. After a few seconds at 4G the force overcame the heart's ability to pump blood up to the brain and the average person lost consciousness. Often this resulted in seizure activity and/or the loss of bladder and bowel control. Recovery could take ten to twenty seconds after the g-force was released. Full awareness and normal function might not come back for several minutes.

When I conducted test flights for the 15th Wing of the RCAF we would routinely pull 7 positive Gs and 3 negative Gs. Every aircraft that required an engine change during maintenance had to be test flown to +7 and -3 Gs. I did a tour as the flight commander for the test pilots, so my schedule included flying three or four different jets on test flights every day. After a few hundred test flights my body adapted to the g-force and my flying style became much more aggressive in order to maximize my productivity.

The test pilots usually flew solo, but newly minted lieutenants would ocsasionally be invited to come along for the experience. A full-card air test was a brutal ride for a new pilot. We only accepted them for less risky test flights, or when we didn't have a full schedule. Several of these new pilots couldn't handle the excessive g-forces or the rapid climbs and descents that were part of our daily routine. Toward the end of the flight, they would respectfully ask me go easy for a few minutes so they could recover.

While at test flight I was tasked by the base medical team to become a pilot for the airsickness program. The program was designed to assist academically gifted students who experienced difficulty with motion sickness and g-force. One promising young student was close to being expelled from pilot training because of motion sickness, particularly when the aircraft rolled into a turn. My task was to work with him over several days until he could tolerate sixty degrees of bank and 2Gs.
On our first flight I asked if we could delay the mission so I could fly over

Buffalo Pound Lake in Saskatchewan to check on my boat. I had loaned my supercharged, high-performance speedboat to a friend and wanted to make sure he was behaving himself with it. The lake was full of boats so I said, "You fly and I'll try to spot it on the water." He circled over the lake and I told him to reverse the turn back over the lake so I could check the southwest shoreline. He did, and I told him to turn harder as the boat came into view. I said, "Now I can see it. Let's head back to base."

He didn't question my decision to land but once we were back on the ground he said he felt fine and asked why I cut the lesson short. I dissected the flight over the lake and reviewed the position of the aircraft after each of my commands. At that moment he realized my command to turn hard over the lake put us slightly over 90 degrees of bank. He was officially cured! He was at the controls and felt fine even at 90 degrees of bank. The problem was a feeling of helplessness when he wasn't flying, and an instructor was at the controls.

The Tough Case

I remember one aircraft technician who thought he was really tough and claimed to be immune to g-force and airsickness. He ridiculed anybody who felt queasy after riding along for a test flight and tormented them mercilessly. I witnessed some of the abuse, and invited this technician along for a test flight. I bet him twenty dollars that if he flew with me on any normal test-flight profile he wouldn't last ten minutes. G tolerance is like sea legs. I told him it didn't matter how tough or how strong you were, it was more an issue of experience and adaptation. Put a tough, muscular landlubber on a ship during a storm and they would feel sick whereas a slender but experienced sailor would be fine.

The morning of the test flight I told him he would love the first ten minutes because I wanted to show him how enjoyable flying could be. After those ten minutes I would perform the full-card air test as if I were flying alone. Test pilots fly much more aggressively when alone so I predicted he would get sick twenty minutes into the flight. He continued to boast, despite my warnings, and proved me wrong. A mere three minutes into the full-card test he became violently ill. I paused the test flight and flew straight and level to let him recover, but when he did, he lied and said he was never sick. Okay, fair enough, so I continued with the air test.

Within two minutes he was convulsing, and wretching violently, and screaming for me to land. No problem. For his own safety I was done with him and already returning to land. Dozens of technicians were waiting for us to taxi in and we parked directly in front of the maintenance hangar.

The technician with me was so weak he couldn't stand up or get out of the aircraft without assistance. He wobbled his way into the maintenance hangar and told everybody he was fine. He wasn't going to pay the twenty dollars because he told them he didn't get sick.

I walked over and burst the airsickness bag he had hidden in his pocket. The result was an instant stench of vomit and a large stain through his flight suit. At that point I announced that I had flown with thousands of students, technicians, and passengers but this guy was the only person who was ever actively airsick with me.

He later admitted he went to a doctor for a prescription to prevent motion sickness. The medication was probably effective for airline travel or riding a roller coaster but all it did was prolong the inevitable. The g-force coupled with rapid changes in altitude completely overwhelmed him.

Barralong Unique Features

DESIGNER: S. M. Van Der Meer

BUILDERS: Van Dam, Holland

YEAR BUILT: 1972

DIMENSIONS:
LOA	55 feet
LOD	47 feet
LWL	42 feet
BEAM	12.5 feet
DRAFT	5 feet 4 inches
GRT / NRT	22.60 / 17.15 Tons

CONSTRUCTION: Welded Siemens Martin shipbuilding steel, teak walk-round deck on steel, iron keel, clipper bow, raked transom with stern windows, raised privateers aft teak sundeck.

ENGINES: Twin 75 HP Volvo Penta MD21, 4-cylinder diesels, with 2:1 reduction gear. Cruising speed 8 knots, maximum speed 10 knots, fuel consumption 2 gallons per hour.

USEABLE FUEL: 308 imperial gallons or 1,400 litres

FRESH WATER: 264 imperial gallons or 1,200 litres

ELECTRICS: 24-volt DC charged by alternators on the main engines. 12-volt step-down converter, Constavolt battery charger, Espar diesel central heating, auxiliary Honda generator.

STEERING: Wheel steering with hydraulic linkage; inside and outside steering stations; emergency tiller.

SAILS: Roller furling Genoa, Yankee staysail, main and mizzen.

DECK: Electric anchor winch, Danforth and CQR anchors. Main anchor with chain, second anchor with line and chain. Avon life-raft; tender on stainless steel davits with 4HP Honda outboard, stainless rigging, full complement of Goiot halyard and sheet winches, alloy spars including twin staysail booms, club-footed jib boom, two teak deck boxes, four stainless steel fender rings, sundeck freshwater faucet for shower; Dynous inflatable three compartment dingy with keel, solid transom, transom wheels and oars.

NAVIGATION: Neco autopilot with electronic compasses. Sestrel Moore steering compass. B&G Log, Echo Sounder, wind speed and direction indicators, clock and barometer. Sitex 32nm radius radar, VHF, Loran C, Radio Direction Finder, loud hailer, automatic fog horn.

INVENTORY: Includes sail covers, Mediterranean awning, life jackets, safety harnesses, flares, four antique saloon stools, flatware and dishes for eight, fitted sheets, drapes, spreads and carpeting throughout.

Fo'c'sle: Storage and chain locker, anchor hose.

Fwd head: Marine toilet, stainless steel sink, hot and cold fresh water, shower; storage cupboards.

Fwd cabin: Port and starboard berths, hanging locker and storage cupboards and drawers.

Galley: Dining area to port converting to a double berth with cupboards overhead; pressurized hot freshwater heater above stainless-steel sink with auxiliary freshwater foot pump; four burner gas stove with blowout sensors, oven and grill, complete with gas alarm; gas/electric fridge; storage cupboards, drawers and sliding door lockers; two ports with screens.

Saloon: Glassed in all around with tempered shatterproof glass; helmsman's position to port; L-shaped settee with dining table to starboard; radio and navigation area to port; balance to starboard with bar area, gas/electric fridge with storage for glasses and supplies; sliding sunroof.

Aft Stateroom: Double berth, drawers and shelf locker to port; settee, hanging wardrobes and vanity table with mirror to starboard, four ports with screens, raising sun hatch.

Aft ensuite: Marine toilet, vanity with stainless steel sink, hot and cold fresh water, shower, cupboards and port with screen.

Marine Cooling Systems

The *Barralong*'s cooling system consisted of both a freshwater and a saltwater system. Both engines had an isolated freshwater cooling system alongside a saltwater system of heat exchangers. A water pump mounted to the front of each engine constantly circulated a mixture of fresh water and antifreeze throughout the engine similar to an automobile.

The saltwater cooling system drew cold seawater into the boat through a strainer and pumped it around the outside tubes running through the heat exchanger. The warm freshwater was pumped through the engine and then through the heat-exchanger tubes so the cold sea water could absorb the heat and keep the freshwater warm, but not hot.

A thermostat on the freshwater system opened and closed to adjust and maintain an operating temperature of around 180 degrees. The cold seawater absorbed heat as it flowed around the warm freshwater tubes and was continuously pumped overboard. The seawater flowed one way only through the heat exchangers, so it kept clean and free of any engine-room contaminants. A strainer on the saltwater system acted like a filter to strain out any weeds or contaminants that might clog the system.

Radar Visual Synchronization

The best lesson Dad taught me about using marine radars was to create a "visual synchronization." The concept was simple. Use the radar often during perfect daytime weather and closely compare the radar's representation of the coastline to what you actually saw outside. Rocky structures, buildings, sandbars, and navigation buoys all reflected radar waves differently and had different characteristics on the radar screen.

By repeatedly comparing the radar picture with the actual coastline, the eye was trained to create a mental image of what the coastline actually looked like just from a glance at the radar screen. In dense fog, maritime chart data and radar data helped to create an accurate mental visualization of surroundings. Add in the water depth information from a depth finder and a three-dimensional image of surroundings was formed.

Mastering the visual synchronization technique assumed that the radar was tuned properly. Early radars in the 1980s weren't as sophisticated, or idiot proof, as modern radars. They had gain, sea state, and range-control dials that had to be manually fine-tuned to achieve good pictures. Most recreational boaters never read manuals or took the time in good weather to learn how to tune the radar. They only turned it on during foggy weather or at night, which could be scary, because they couldn't tune it fast enough or visualize what the radar screen tried to tell them.

During beautiful weather, the visual synchronization concept taught how each manual-tuning knob affected the radar-scope results. Sea state was a good example. The radar beam was sent out from a magnetron mounted high up on the mast. The sea state control raised and lowered the radar beam above the surface of the water. If the wave heights were big and the beam was set too low, the radar beam struck the tops of the waves and made it look as though a vessel was surrounded.

If the beam were set too high it would not reflect off of a low sandbar or a small boat. Similarly, if the sea-state setting was too high, a charted navigation buoy would be very difficult to find because the radar beam passed above the buoy without striking it. If the beam didn't strike the buoy, it couldn't reflect back to the receiver.

Navigation and Log Keeping

Ancient mariners made their way from A to B in a zigzag fashion because sailing vessels couldn't advance straight into the wind. Modern sailing vessels are more efficient but still have to zigzag toward their destination. In the days before GPS each series of zigs and zags had to be carefully recorded in a logbook so the navigator could determine their new position. As you can imagine, this was a difficult thing to do when at sea for several weeks at a time and out of sight from land.

Navigation required determining a boat's speed in each zig and zag for a given length of time. Ancient mariners measured boat speed by throwing a piece of wood next to the bow and counting how long it took to reach the stern. Around four hundred years ago sailors increased the accuracy by using a long rope with knots tied in it at fifty-foot intervals. A piece of wood was tied to the end of the rope and it was thrown overboard behind the ship. As the ship traveled forward, the piece of wood pulled the rope and the knots into the water. The crew would start a primitive, thirty-second "egg timer" and count how many knots passed over the stern in thirty seconds. The faster the ship was moving, the more knots were pulled overboard, and the measure of speed was called "knots." If four knots were pulled into the water in thirty seconds, the boat was traveling 200 feet in thirty seconds, which translated into 24,000 feet in an hour. A nautical mile was approximately 6,000 feet, so a speed of 24,000 feet in an hour meant four nautical miles per hour. Ten knots meant ten nautical miles per hour.

Remember those Navy contracts Dad negotiated to help offset the *Barralong*'s expenses? They required that young Navy cadets be taught the fundamentals of navigation without the aid of electronic devices. As part of the curriculum, each cadet helped to prepare logbook entries to keep track of the ship's progress. Here are two excerpts from the *Barralong*'s logbook created by the cadets.

Diesel Filters and Injectors

Diesel fuel is far less volatile than gasoline and must be pressurized or atomized in order to burn. Toss a match into a bucket of diesel fuel

SHIP'S LOG — CADET SUMMER TRAINING OPERATION

S/Y BARRALONG 1990

VOYAGE FROM: East Bay
TO: Sydney N.S.
CAPTAIN: Ian G. Stott
OFFICERS: Joe Mombourquette
2nd Officer Robin Campbell
2nd Officer Robin Campbell 1st Watch
DATE: July 1/91
CREW: —

Fuel 42"
Water Full

Rotating hourly watches / Rotating 1/2 hourly

Time	Revs	Speed	Bar.	Temp.	Wind	W/Sp.	Course	Log	Position
0755	2100	7kt	29.6	52°	NE	22	240°		45°05'81"N 60°32'72"W Raining Blustery
0830	2100	7kt	29.6	52	NE	22	240		Eskasoni Church Abeam
1136	2100	7kt	29.6	62°	NE	8	72°		Kidston Island Lighthouse Abeam
1232	2100	7kts	29.5	66°	NE	10	85°		Big Harbour Entrance Buoy Abeam
1305	2100	6.5kts	29.5	64°	NE	11kts	85°		Man of War Point Stbd Abeam Calm & Sunny
1341	2100	7kts	29.5	62°	NE	14	85°		Passed Under Seal Island Bridge Clear & Sunny
1422	2100	8.5kts	29.5	62°	NE	14	70°		Black Rock Lighthouse Abeam
1615	2000	7.5	29.5	59°	SE	12	240		Cranberry Hd Buoy Abeam

COURSE #1 — DEPT NATIONAL DEFENCE CHARTER — Royal Canadian Sea Cadets "Louisburg 384"

CRUISE FROM: East Bay, St Peters Canal, TO: Descousse, St Peters, Baddeck, East Bay
DATE: July 3-4-5/87 No. OF TRAINEES ABOARD: 4
CREW: Lt Peterson Lt Brown
OWNER: Capt Ian G. Stott

Date	#	Time Departed	Port Departed From: Buoy, Landmarks or Other	Log Reading	Course Steered	Distance	Magnetic	Motor R.P.M.s	Estimated Speed	Estimated Time To Next Objective	Arrival Time	Place Arrived At
July 3	1	1218	Abeam E3	8379	252°			2000	8kts	3.20	1540	Tied up St Peters Lock
July 3	2	1600	Dep St Peters Canal	—				2000	8kts	.50	1700	Tied up Descousse
July 4	3	0830	Dep Descousse	—				2000	8kts	.50	0900	Tied up St Peters Canal
	4	0930	Dep St Peters Canal					2000	8kts	4 hrs	1400	Tied up Baddeck
	5	0900	Dep Baddeck					2000	8kts	4 hrs	1600	via Maskell Hbr Iona, Benacadie Hd
	6	1300	Dep Iona					2000	8kts	3 hrs	1604	Arr East Bay

REMARKS: Trainees Aboard
8-AA/8-A/1-BA
1-AA/16A/1-BA
1-AA/15A/3 BA
14 AA/5 A

NAME	ADDRESS OR TELEPHONE
A/B Ken Ley	RR1 Louisburg Dave & Judy Ley
Able Seaman Ron Ward	RR1 Louisburg Charles & Elsie Ward
Leading Cadet Donnie Wadden	Trout Brook Road Louisburg
Leading Cadet Jody Kennedy	RR2 Marion Bridge Lucy Kennedy

Fuel Supplied CFS Sydney
Food Supplied CFS Sydney

and it will go out, but toss a match into a bucket of flammable liquid like gasoline and it will blow your head off. Flammable liquids ignite easily whereas diesel is considered combustible rather than flammable. Combustible liquids are not as reactive to an open flame and therefore safer to handle.

Instead of a spark plug, diesel engines use devices called injectors to pressurize a tiny mist of fuel into each cylinder about 2,000 times per minute. The problem with injectors is that they are very susceptible to water and dirt particles. When a diesel-engine fuel-filtration system gets clogged the engine immediately quits due to fuel starvation. The only way to restart the engine is to unclog or replace the filter(s). When a fuel filter is replaced, air gets introduced into the system. The process to remove any trapped air or water from the fuel injector system is called "bleeding the injectors." If the trapped air or water isn't properly purged, a diesel engine won't start.

To bleed an injector, the bleed screw must be opened from a kneeling position beside the engine while the starter is engaged. Opening the bleed screw allows the air and water to escape. The fuel system is sealed again by closing the bleed screw just before the starter is disengaged. It sounds like a relatively easy task but when filters get clogged during a storm at sea it's because the boat is being tossed around violently. During a voyage the engine room is a very hot, stinky, and dangerous place at the best of times.

The *Barralong*'s engines were very close together so it was scary to have one engine thrashing away at high RPM while trying to bleed the injectors on the dead engine beside it. One rogue wave slammed up against the hull was all it would take to throw me into the scalding hot exhaust manifold or a spinning propeller shaft. It was a cramped place, so the trick was to tightly wedge myself into position between the bulkheads. One hand stayed free to bleed the injectors but every limb including my head, was wedged against something to tightly secure my position.

Patti, Barney, and Glenn

Acknowledgements

Writing a book is much harder than I thought. I certainly couldn't have done it without the countless hours my beautiful wife Patti dedicated to helping with story ideas, proofreading, and evaluating text.

To Elaine Ash, sister, master editor, creative motivator, and publishing mentor; your leadership and guidance gave the story life and made finishing this entire project possible. And to Albert Tucher, Principal Librarian Emeritus of the Newark Public Library, for your expertise.

To Brean Stott, my brother and business partner, you are the source of many hilarious childhood stories told here. Thanks for your help and trust in putting the *Barralong* voyage together.

To my brother Ian, for cheering me on in support of putting these words onto paper. You are missed.

To Colin MacDonald, first mate and spectacular marine chef, for staying strong in the face of high seas and adversity. To Mark Ferris, Terry Keating, and Mike Sassco for sharing the dream.

To Gary Hof, Suzzanne Miller, and Sean Holland for your friendship and calm professionalism during extremely challenging conditions.

To the boys; Frank Cousineau, Paul Quinn, Bob Simmons, Marv MacAuley, and Rick Ellerbrok for your support and sage advice.

To Steve Teatro—friend, master mariner, and international skipper of the Jabiroo II—for your friendship and expertise. Thanks a million.

To our father, Ian G. Stott, for his pursuit of excellence, and inspiring his children to forge ahead through adversity.

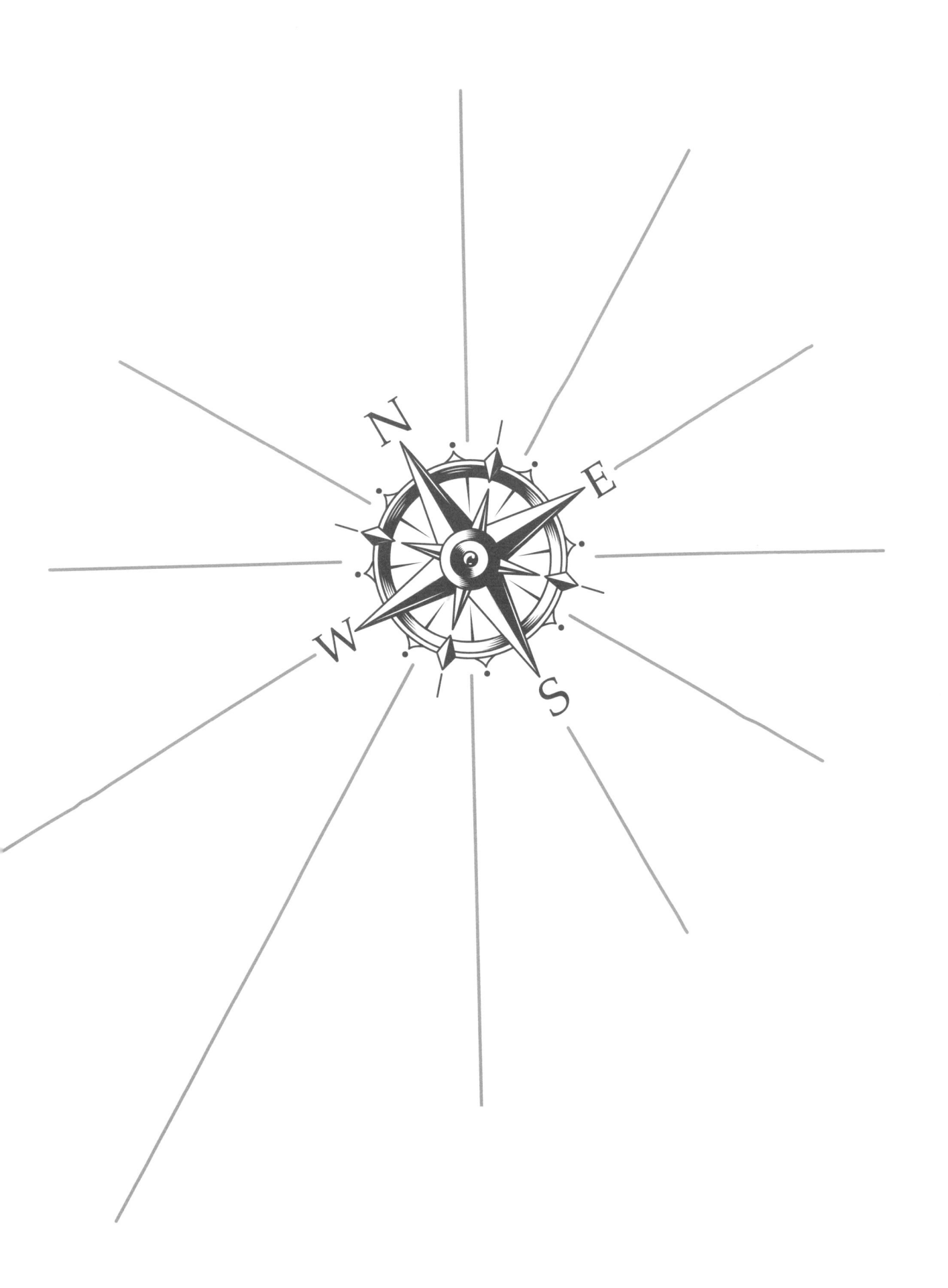

Please add any thoughts or memories here so they can be preserved and passed along with this book.

Please add any thoughts or memories here so they can be preserved and passed along with this book.

Made in the USA
Columbia, SC
01 July 2024